# KARATE

*Parting The Clouds With Empty Hands*

# KARATE: Parting The Clouds With Empty Hands

## Copyright Garry Lever 2012

All rights reserved. No part of this book may be reproduced without the express written permission of the copyright owner.

**Photographs** All photographs contained within this publication are from the personal collection of the author unless otherwise stated. No photographs may be reproduced in either printed or electronic format without the prior written permission of the author.

Published by Garry Lever London 2012

ISBN: 978-1-4716-4499-3

## Disclaimer

The author of this book will not be held responsible in any manner whatsoever for any injury that may result from practicing the techniques and/or instructions given within. Since the physical activities described may be too strenuous in nature for some readers to engage in safely, it is essential that a physician be consulted prior to training

## Cover Art

Photography courtesy of Gary Lever Snr. Calligraphy *'karate no kokoro'* by Hokama Tetsuhiro *sensei* from the private collection of the author.

*For Joshua*

# Contents

| | |
|---|---|
| Foreword – by Glyn Jones *Renshi* | 8 |
| Introduction | 10 |
| If You Ain't Fighting, You Ain't Doing Karate | 13 |
| One Size Doesn't Fit All | 15 |
| Life And Death In Okinawa | 17 |
| Not Tense But Firm | 20 |
| In Car Self Defense | 22 |
| Listen….Do You Want To Know A Secret? | 24 |
| Go And Ju Eye Methods | 27 |
| Could You Learn From This Teacher? | 31 |
| Take Care Of Your Health | 33 |
| Osoji | 35 |
| Letting Go | 37 |
| Two Big Diseases | 40 |
| Teaching Methods | 44 |
| More On Miyagi Sensei's Self Defense Methods | 48 |
| The Dojo | 50 |
| Be Polite | 54 |
| The Real Meaning Of Bunkai | 56 |
| Before And After The Battle | 60 |
| Kata According To The Elements | 63 |
| Eggs | 72 |
| Jishin | 74 |
| Hitting The Target | 77 |
| Accepting Criticism | 81 |
| Using The Kata | 83 |
| Balanced Training | 89 |
| The Performance Of Kata | 92 |

| | |
|---|---|
| The Cycle Of The Sun & Moon | 96 |
| Leaving Things Better | 98 |
| A Zen Experience | 100 |
| Busaganashi | 103 |
| Karatedo & Healing | 105 |
| Advanced Punching Ideas | 112 |
| Teaching And Perception | 115 |
| Stealing The Initiative | 119 |
| Go & Ju Of Conflict Management | 123 |
| Animal Methods In Goju Ryu | 127 |
| Okinawa 2011 | 134 |
| An Interview With Richard Barrett Sensei | 174 |
| Personal Formation Through A Study Of Karate-Do | 185 |
| Conclusion | 191 |

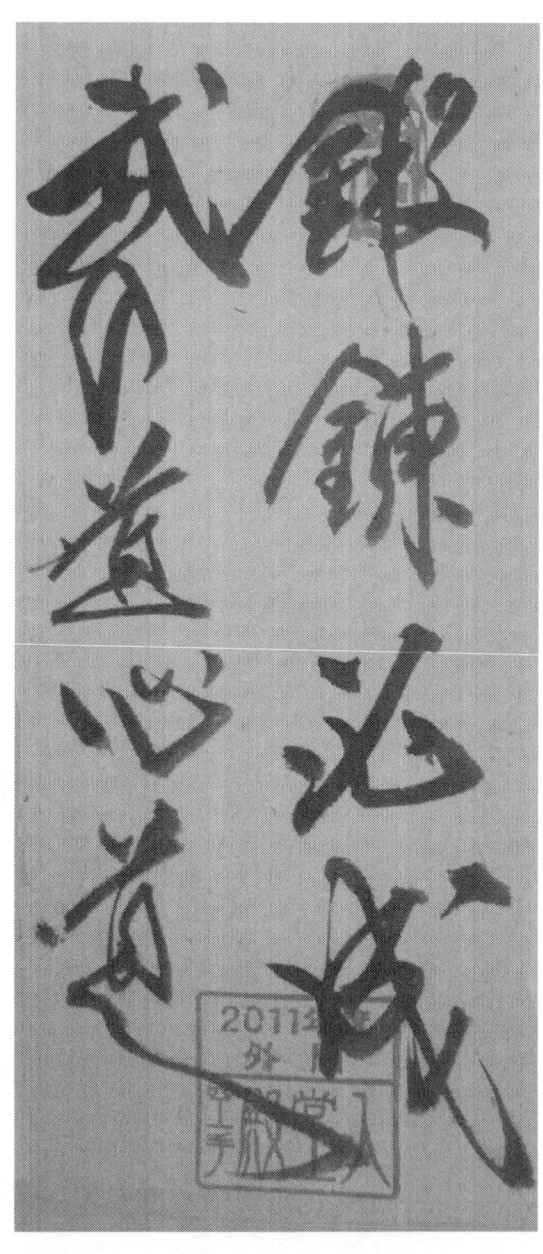

*Budo is a path of your heart, training leads you to completion*

*Hokama Tetshuiro sensei*

*Daruma and Kyu Do Mugen brushed by Hokama Tetsuhiro sensei*

# Foreword

by Glyn Jones *Renshi*

On an idyllic group of islands in the south pacific, the peaceful people of *Okinawa* have for centuries been practising an indigenous little art known as *Karate*. An art that was quietly passed on through the generations by its people by way of a close teacher to student relationship; a mutual bond based on loyalty, honour, and respect. The true *Karate* of *Okinawa* with its inner codes of courtesy and etiquette was an art that was always practised diligently and quietly without any need for fuss or external gratification from outsiders. To receive quality guidance from a *Sensei* of deep understanding, together with the many benefits gained from regular hard practise, were the only real rewards on offer for their lifelong devotion to practising their native art.

Over the past century *Karate* has taken flight around the world, an art that in its beginnings was practised by closer to hundreds on its home land on *Okinawa* prior to making its way to the shores of *Japan*, and in time going on to being practised by millions of people all around the world. Through its journey across many lands and sea, *Karate* achieved much fame and worldwide credited acclaim. What is evident is that through this passage of time, there have been many changes in direction from a *Karate* that was once so distinct and easily defined, to slowly becoming almost unrecognisable at times from the ways of practise that was originally set out by teachers on *Okinawa* of old, with many of *Karate's* core characteristics being totally disregarded or lost along the way.

The word *Karate* has become more of a generic term, with all who practise the art being labelled as one and the same; a labelling that is far from the truth and more than an injustice to the *Karate* men and women of Okinawa. I am therefore more than happy to highly recommend this excellent work by Garry Lever *Sensei*, as it clarifies in detail to all who take the time to read its contents, that there is a vast clear difference in the way that people study and practise the art of *Karate*. What separates the author from the masses is the way in which he studies, practises, and teaches the art of *Karate*, all of which is soon evident upon reading his words by the excellent advice and guidance he openly shares. Lever *Sensei's* way of approaching *Karate* practise is not for everyone, and I'm more than confident in saying that he wouldn't wish it to be either, as his way is not based on training in large numbers, for gaining wealth or higher status, or for winning cups, but by quietly practising in a way that is more common to the people of Okinawa, a *Karate* that is full of substance that requires much commitment and a deeper understanding. One may simply call this *Budo*.

Many of the elder more senior *Karate Sensei* on *Okinawa,* including my own teacher, as in Shigetoshi Senaha *Sensei*, have growing concerns for the future of their native art, believing that more of the true teachings of *Okinawan Karate* are being lost or diluted with each and every generation, believing that authentic *Karate* is becoming more rare and harder to seek out with every new decade that passes by. However, even though quality guidance may be on the decline and to the sincere student it can feel like searching for a diamond on a beach of sand, there is a glimmer of light and much hope for both the serious *Karate* student, and for the longevity of the art itself, all of which is due to those *Sensei* like the author, who wish to preserve and promote *Karate* in its more original form without dilution.

**"Parting the Clouds with Empty Hands"** is a work that I whole heartedly recommend to all who are serious about studying *Karate*. I not only feel that this book will offer guidance and give direction to both the beginner and more advanced *Karate* exponent of many years, it is also a great read and valued reference material. There are just so many excellent writings and articles contained within like *"Osoji"* to name one of many, all of which will make the reader richer for the experience for reading it.

The guidance that Garry Lever *Sensei* continues to receive from his own teacher as in Richard Barrett *Sensei*, together with the loyalty he shows, deep respect for, and high regard that he has for his *Sensei* just shines through when reading this book, it is a *Karate* that is based on a close teacher to student relationship, which is not only the original way, but also the most beneficial approach to transmitting the true teachings of the *Okinawn* art of *Karate*.

**Glyn Jones  *Renshi*  6th Dan**
**Ryusyokai Okinawa Goju -Ryu Karate**
**Ilfracombe, England.**

# Introduction

*'Part the clouds, seek the way'*

This advice was passed on by Funakoshi Gichin *sensei* to all aspiring students of *karatedo*, and I can think of no phrase better suited to describing how this art is best approached. With so many distractions seemingly attached to *budo* these days, I sometimes wish we could all return to the days when likeminded practitioners would gather together and train just for the sake of training rather than the current prevailing spirit of one-upmanship. It seems as though somehow we've managed to create something very complicated out of that which was originally very simple. This is human nature I guess and is not something which is limited only to *karate*.

It appears to be the case that many people are somehow attracted to the distractions and actively collect them by concerning themselves too much with trivial matters such as rank, titles, number of followers, recognition, or association with a famous teacher. These are just some of the more tangible clouds which need to be parted before the serious business of training can be allowed to begin; but just like the clouds in the sky, there are many different layers which you have to pass through before being treated to a glimpse of clarity. This first layer of distractions is actually fairly easy to part; you simply have to decide to have nothing to do with such matters, for they are all things which can easily be removed or avoided from your life.

Some people have commented to me that they wish their training could be as simple as mine; not having to worry about memberships, associations or rent, etc. My response is always the same; make it that simple. I am not a rich man but I do have the mind-set required to put my life in order and cut out anything which is non-essential so that I can enjoy doing the things that I love and avoid those which make me unhappy. I train and teach out of a tiny *dojo* in the rear garden of my family home which means I do not have to worry about *dojo* fees, memberships, number of students or even retaining the few that I have. If they were to all decide one day that *karate* wasn't for them and choose to leave my *dojo*, I would continue training the following day, the same way as I always do. The few students I do have are there because they have earned my trust and are sincere in their efforts; because of this we are compatible. I do not have to waste my time on people who are looking for entertainment which means I also don't need to worry about advertising or creating a name for myself by aligning myself with famous teachers or selling my art. This is a very simple approach, but one which is not embraced by many people because almost everybody has an excuse for why it wouldn't be possible in their circumstances.

You see, there is a big difference between **studying** *karatedo* as *budo*, and **practising** *karate* as recreation. *Budo karate* has to be taught as *budo*; there is no shortcut to this and no easy route. *Karate* as recreation is what most people want; although most will adamantly state that they want *budo karate*. What is the difference? This is something which I hope the various articles contained in this book might be able to shed some light upon, and help to raise a few questions in your mind about your current approach to the art.

*Budo* will never be something for the masses; it is far too personal, intimate and confrontational for that, and I think it is the confrontation more than anything else which causes most people to find an alternative. Defeating an opponent is not such a difficult task, and this is why many people who are concerned only with the physical in the martial arts can easily convince themselves and other people that they are studying *budo*. The confrontation that *budo* provides is not with an external opponent, but with your own true nature. I realise that this will sound very cliché, but unfortunately it is the truth. Perhaps it would be appropriate here to mention briefly about my background in order to provide a little context to some of the views you are about to read, otherwise they could be easily dismissed as lacking credibility.

I have worked in Law Enforcement for many years with the majority of my service being spent on a specialist unit which deals with large scale public disorder, gang violence and individuals who are considered too dangerous for regular officers to safely deal with. I have experienced everything from single opponents to group attacks and full scale riot. I have been attacked with weapons, threatened with firearms, been outnumbered by multiple opponents and have first-hand knowledge of the strong emotions which are encountered through such incidents. I mention this not to boast about my fighting prowess, for I feel that my ability in this regard is mediocre at best. I mention it because I understand a little about how authentic *budo* training can help prepare the body and spirit to help you move forward when every bone in your body is telling you to curl up and hide. This has a far greater range of application than the mere act of fighting.

Through my experiences so far, I recognise now that any confrontation is actually an encounter with my true self; the one that quietly hides away most of the time and only comes out to annoy me and interfere during the occasions when I actually require calmness and clarity in my mind. No matter how skilled you become at presenting an image to the outside world, the true self will always be able to see through it and emerge occasionally to remind you he's still there. The challenge in *budo* lies in coming to terms with this 'true self' and confronting it regularly so that you can learn to control it. Studying *karatedo* provides us with the means of confronting this demon and the *dojo* can be considered the battleground where this war is fought. The true self is the voice that tells you 'you're scared' or 'you can't do this'. He's the one that tries to prevent you from achieving you goals and stop you from advancing further in life. The negative voices which appear are the next layer of clouds that need to be parted in your training and the empty hands are the tools at your disposal. These clouds are much more elusive than the previous ones though and you will need to pay greater attention in order to notice them. I've yet to completely part these clouds for myself as I am still fully engaged in my personal battle, but I hope that one day I might get an opportunity to glimpse clarity for a little while.

# If You Ain't Fighting, You Ain't Doing Karate

**Kumite** at the Kenshikan *dojo*

I received an email out of the blue one day, arriving during a period of my life where I had been involved in a number of altercations at work. The nature of the conflicts I was engaged in might not what you imagine straight away though, for much of the battle was being fought within the confines of my own conscience. I had been required to do things and make split second decisions in the heat of the moment which, with hindsight, may have been wrong and against my beliefs. Following an altercation I'm always faced with many days of second guessing my actions and questioning whether I could have resolved things in a better way. Ultimately, what's done is done and cannot be changed, however; this does little to reconcile the conscience when you have hurt another person. The email in question was from my *sensei*, and there was a particular part of it which hit home like a bolt of lightning. It made mention of the word soul, and how when we are training in the *dojo* we should be coming face to face with our own true nature.

There is a particular saying *'Ikken nyu kon'* which Higashionna Kanryo *sensei* was believed to be particularly fond of which roughly means *'a fist that penetrates the soul'*. On one occasion when I was visiting my teacher at his home in Spain he had me draw this phrase a number of times, trying to reveal the essence of the characters through the strokes of the brush. I found this a difficult thing to do as I'm still trying to fully understand what the soul is. When I first read this phrase it conjured up an image in my mind of training the body in order to build a technique strong enough to stop an opponent; to penetrate and break their spirit, securing victory. I now think of this quite differently and no longer believe the phrase has anything to do with any external opponent at all.

I find it particularly distasteful to read of *karate* in terms of 'scrapping' or fighting. There is nothing more degrading and sad than seeing two grown adults fight. I find *karateka* who concern themselves too much with this quite embarrassing, as if they are trying to justify the art to other people somehow. There is genius in the saying *'do not strike others, do not be struck by others, this is the principle of peace without incident'*. It is a great shame when *karateka* are forced to use their techniques to defend themselves, although it would appear that many eagerly want to test their skills for real judging by what is often written these days.

If you have been taught *karate* as *budo*, you will probably already have an idea in your head about the kind of character you should be working towards possessing. The person you display to the outside world will often be different to the person who is shown to close friends and family. This will also most likely be quite different to the person who you really are; the true self. Perhaps this is the actual meaning of *Sanchin* 'three conflicts'?

By using *karate* as a means of doing battle with our own souls we have a very powerful tool when it comes to personal development, but this is only the case if we have the courage to actually face ourselves daily rather than hiding away from our true nature, pretending it isn't there. If you conveniently choose to ignore the parts of your character which you dislike, you are walking the path of a coward. You are backing down from the one fight in your life where *karatedo* can help you the most.

This particular kind of training is not confined to the *dojo*. It is a battle which will last your whole life, for a significant part of your waking hours. Perhaps the battle becomes easier as you mature, but at the moment I'm personally bracing myself for a long campaign. So the next time somebody asks you 'have you ever had to use *karate* in a fight' you can answer 'yes, every day'.

*Gambatte*!

# One Size Doesn't Fit All

Whenever you read about how *karate* was practiced long ago, frequently we find that students were taught according to their individual requirements, with techniques and *kata* being modified according to the student. This is a long way from today's rigid set standards brought about by *karate's* integration with mainland Japanese *budo* and the emergence of sports *karate*, where every technique has to be performed according to a specific model to ensure that we are all doing the same thing. Such methods allow little space for individuality or personal growth and completely neglect a student's personal circumstances. Often, if a particular technique doesn't work, it is not the fault of the technique, but rather the fault of the student who is yet to discover a way of making it work for themselves. A teacher can assist in this process by advising a slight change of angle, or how to apply the same technique to a different target area, etc.

Having said that, it is a tricky subject as often things can be changed with the best intentions in mind, but without a good understanding of the principles behind a technique, a change can occur to the detriment of the art and the student. In fact I think the word change itself is unsuitable, for to change something often means that something also gets lost. To specialize or to adapt would perhaps be a more appropriate term. This implies making something your own, taking ownership. This is what I think we should be trying to achieve in our training, to take ownership of our art and to assume responsibility for our own development.

The *kata* remain the constant. These do not change, but the actual use of the *kata* techniques is completely individual. A lighter student will not be picking up and body slamming a heavy opponent, and a heavier student might not necessarily have the light, quick footwork required to dart in and out of range, and so might have to specialize in engaging an opponent from a very close range to overwhelm them with strength. For this reason, the same technique will be applied slightly differently by each person according to their unique strengths and weaknesses.

As a student of *karatedo* it is important to look in-depth at your own strengths and weaknesses, for these will dictate your use of the *kata*. This is why people were assigned certain *kata* for their individual study in the old days. A strong student might be given *seiunchin* which favors staying at close range and unbalancing an opponent, whereas a lighter student might be assigned *saifa* which prefers disengaging and getting out of the way.

In the early stages of our training we should of course endeavor to become equally competent at all areas of our art, but as we progress we might find ourselves naturally drifting toward certain parts of practice. I personally enjoy *kakie* the most and this would probably be my area of specialization. Others may favor *hojo undo*, conditioning or perhaps *kata*.

Aside from body types, physical restrictions will also dictate how we use our art. Injuries that we pick up throughout life or natural disabilities are an important consideration. If a person has suffered a shoulder injury in the past and lacks the sufficient shoulder flexibility to attain the perfect chamber position of the fist in *Sanchin*, what is the point in forcing it to the extent of destroying the rest of the structure? We have to figure out exactly how close we can get to this ideal before the shoulder begins to rise, or the elbow loses connection with the body. The important thing is the structural integrity of the technique rather than the perfect photograph worthy end position.

Having said this, we shouldn't become lazy and make excuses for our shortcomings. I was always so impressed to see Kinjo Seikichi *sensei* training at the *Jundokan dojo*. In his 70's and still training regularly, Kinjo *sensei* had a permanent shake to one of his arms caused by a *judo* accident in his youth. He was always very apologetic about this, but he really didn't need to be. He had lived with this impairment for the majority of his life and learnt to overcome it, to the extent that he would quite easily dominate during *sandan gi* and *kakie* practice even though I was a young, fit 20 year old in my prime! I'm full of admiration for this great *karateka*. Poor old Kinjo *sensei* would have probably scored zero points at a *kata* tournament, but he sure as heck knew how to use his *karate*!

*Karatedo* is very much a study of people. When we consider how different we all are, how can we ever claim to know everything about our art? Each student brings with them a unique challenge and it is up to the teacher to help them discover how to use their art according to their own personality and body type most effectively. By going through this process, the teacher is able to learn the intricate details of the art and discover the infinite possibilities available within each technique. On a physical level, this is the meaning of *kyu do mugen*, 'there is no end to seeking the way'.

# Life And Death In Okinawa

Modern turtleback style tomb of Hanashiro Chomo *sensei* in Shuri

Some of the most striking images in Okinawa for me are the turtleback style tombs which can be found in various locations around the island. They appear as imposing grand structures, and are no doubt very expensive which should give some indication about the importance placed upon honoring deceased family members in Ryukyu culture.

Ancestor worship is considered very important in Okinawa, which does not have any state religion. When you think of Thailand you think Buddhism, Japan Shinto, England Christianity, etc. Okinawa does not have this as such, but this does not mean it is devoid of spirituality; they just prefer to keep things a little closer to home and more personal. Of course, many religions have influenced Okinawan culture greatly but the individual practices of the islanders most commonly reflect a deep respect toward ones ancestors and nature in general.

The turtleback tombs were introduced to Okinawa from China, although I'm not sure whether the folklore attached to them is Chinese in origin or more native to Ryukyu. In Okinawa the turtleback tomb is believed to represent the concept of 'mother'. The large bump on the top characterizes the womb, the vertical pillars at the front the legs, and the opening, the vagina. In short, we emerge onto the earth from the mother, and upon leaving the earth we return to that same source[1]. It is easy to see the parallels between the Okinawan use of the term mother and the Chinese concept of *Dao*.

On the floor, close to the opening of the tomb will be a small structure where the 'spirit' of the tomb's guardian resides. When paying ones respects it is important to first acknowledge this guardian by bowing toward it, asking permission to approach the tomb. If the tomb is particularly grand and features a surrounding wall it is also considered correct etiquette to bow before entering this area and also upon leaving, as you would in the *dojo*. The burning of incense is believed to attract the spirits who enjoy the smell, and this is the same with offerings of food or drink. The Okinawans believe that such gestures help to bring the spirits of their departed relatives closer so that they can spend a little time with them once again. Death is not usually considered the end of a relationship, for this relationship continues after the spirit has left the body through such customs as *Obon*.

In the *dojo* it is common to see a small container on the *shinzen*. This container might sometimes contain some of the ashes of the *sensei's* own teacher, and it is considered a great honor to be trusted with such a treasure. In the case of the Hokama *dojo* there are two small urns on the *shinzen*, one containing some of ashes of Higa Seiko *sensei*, and the other, Fukuchi Seiko *sensei*. When bowing toward the *shinzen*, this gives it extra importance and helps keep one's teachers close during training. Students of the *Jundokan dojo* are particularly lucky for they have inherited the training equipment of Miyagi Chojun *shinshi*. The handles of the equipment are literally ingrained with the dead skin and sweat of the founder of *Goju Ryu*. This builds a close relationship with the lineage of the art and a personal link to the history.

For many people lineage is not considered important, but I'm not so sure. I'm not disagreeing from a snobbish point of view, implying that if you haven't trained through direct channels to the founder of your respective art you can't understand it properly. So long as the training practices are passed on carefully and correctly this is not so important. What is important though, is developing a personal relationship with your art. This leads to an appreciation of the history, a respect for your teachers, and a determination to play your part in ensuring its correct transmission to the next generation.

If you tell a new student they must bow upon entering the *dojo*, they will do it. If you do not explain why they are doing it though, they will

---

[1] Discussion with Hokama Tetsuhiro, Shuri, Okinawa 2011

perform the physical action without the necessary emotional content and it then becomes empty and pointless. This same idea continues to other areas of training so that *kata* practice become empty and pointless, *soji* becomes empty and pointless, it **all** becomes pointless and then the art has no value. This, I fear, is what has happened in most *karate dojo* around the world. Give something a purpose and it will retain value and be cherished. I think that the people teaching *karatedo* have a big responsibility to explain more to their students. It also requires greater dedication from the student to always ask why. This doesn't mean to bother your *sensei* with endless questions, but to ask yourself why and conduct your own research.

Through practicing *karatedo* you have inherited a history and a family. I think it is a good thing to say thank you for this by whatever means you can. If you can visit the tomb of your teachers, this is a great thing. If this is not possible though, the least you can do is follow the tradition to the best of your ability and say thank you to them through the correct performance of *Rei*.

**Ancient turtleback style tomb of *Bojutsu* master Gusukuma in Sueyoshi**

# Not TENSE But Firm!!!!

**The giant rope at the annual Naha O-Tsuna Hiki**

*Sanchin* and *Goju Ryu* seem to have this problem where they cannot be discussed by practitioners of other styles for very long before the terms 'tension' and 'forced breathing' appear in the conversation. The discussion then usually goes on to include the phrases 'high blood pressure' and the associated 'health problems'. The frustrating thing is this does not only happen with inexperienced practitioners, but also with many high ranking and well researched authorities in Okinawa!

Look, if you play soccer using a rock instead of the air inflated ball which everybody else uses, it will lead to health problems. If you practice your butterfly swimming technique on the concrete floor instead of the swimming pool, it will lead to health problems. If you practice your archery skills by jabbing yourself in the eye with the arrow, guess what, it will lead to health problems.

*Sanchin* should not be tense. It does not use 'dynamic tension', and in fact, I do not know what that phrase is even supposed to mean. The very word tension annoys me, and if it used when teaching it conveys completely the wrong idea to the student and destroys their *karate* in the long run. Tension can be likened to flooring the gas on your car whilst stamping on the footbrake at the same time. This is not good for the car and will not get you to where you are supposed to be travelling. Tension on a physical level leads to even more tension on an emotional level, making the student a nervous wreck. They become very jumpy, stuttery and hesitant. None of their moves will be natural and there will be a massive gap between thought and action. This is quite painful to watch.

But, *Sanchin* should also not be relaxed. It is like a bow string which is pulled back part way to allow for the quick release of the arrow should a threat suddenly appear. It is like having a finger ready on the trigger with part of the pressure already taken up when firing a pistol. It is ready, it is engaged; it is the sprinter on the blocks, poised and waiting for the 'go' so that they can beat their opponent to the finish line.

*Sanchin* is not tense, but *Sanchin* **is** firm. This is not a contradiction. Tense is the arms shaking, excessive sweating, seeing stars, the face going red and about to explode. Firm does not show anything to the observer, but is something which they can feel for themselves.

This firmness is not achieved through actively engaging muscle groups, but by linking together the different parts of the body through opposite rotations. This can be compared to the strands of a rope which entangle in order to provide the rope with its strength. If all the strands ran parallel in the same direction, the rope would be weaker than by having them overlap and weaving together. This is the same with the body structure in *Sanchin*. How is this learnt? Through *hojo undo* and hands-on correction from a *sensei* who understands *Sanchin*.

With regards to the breathing, the sound made during *Sanchin* is not an intentional act but is something which occurs as a result of the right things happening. The breathing should be audible, but not forced. The breathing should be deep, but not strained. It should not be from the throat. It should not sound like you have a chest infection. The breathing should be in time with the movements of the body so that there is no discernible gap between thought, breath, and action. The breathing should feel as though you are cleansing your whole body, rather than trying to drag a rose bush through your lungs.

A good indication as to whether you are performing *Sanchin* correctly with regard to muscle use and breathing is how you feel at the end of the *kata*. If you are dizzy and exhausted, you've probably done it wrong. If you feel invigorated and energized, *Sanchin* has done what it was designed to do and you may have just set yourself up to have a great day.

# In Car Self Defense

This is a very sad, but unfortunately true story. The victim was inside his vehicle talking with his girlfriend whilst parked in a quiet side street in a relatively safe area of London. The attacker approached the passenger side door and dragged the victim's girlfriend out of the car, holding a knife and threatening to stab her unless he handed over the keys. The victim responded to this by hiding the keys underneath the driver's seat and the attacker then fatally stabbed him in the chest before driving off in the vehicle, leaving him dead at the scene in front of his terrified girlfriend.

This is a frightening thought. One moment the victim is spending time with his girlfriend, both happy and oblivious to the evil intent of the scumbag who was watching them from close by. The next minute, the victim lies dying and his girlfriend has just watched his brutal murder. The effect that this will have on the victims' loved ones will be impossible for them to ever fully recover from. All of this over a car!

The really sad thing is that a few simple precautions might have given the victim just enough time to escape and save his life.

Many of us when we are inside our vehicles switch off a little. Within the safety of our four metal walls it becomes easy to forget about the outside world whilst we focus on our driving, the music on the radio, the traffic, being late for work, or the idiot who just cut in front of us. It always amuses me when I see people getting angry in their vehicles, shouting at other drivers. These same people would probably never be brave enough to do such a thing if they were outside of the safety bubble of their car where the other person might actually respond to their shouting!

When you go to your car, how do you approach it? Do you look around on your approach to see if anyone is following or watching you? Do you check if the tires are correctly inflated? Do you check through the windows before entering to see if anyone is hiding inside? Once inside, do you lock the doors? On a hot day, how much do you open the window? How often do you check your mirrors and take note of the vehicle following behind? Who is inside that vehicle, and how long have they been behind you? How close do you stop behind the car in front at a red traffic signal or in a queue? What route do you take on your way to and from work, and do you have a regular routine which somebody could take advantage of? Do you have an impressive car which would be attractive to thieves? Is your mobile phone charged and within reach? What is inside the vehicle which could be used to defend yourself with in an emergency? If the car in front suddenly stopped, how could you escape? Who is approaching on the pavement whilst you are stationary in this traffic jam?

These are some of the things I think about naturally whenever I drive. All of this goes on quietly in the background whilst I get on with my everyday activities, and this has even more importance now that I sometimes have my son in the back of the car.

Some parts of London have a particular problem with car-jackings, and a few years ago I was almost the victim of this. I had dropped a friend off at a train station and was driving home when I was stopped by a red traffic signal behind two other cars. Suddenly the passenger door of the car in front swung open and a male got out, running toward my driver's door carrying a weapon. Luckily I had left enough space in front to be able to quickly maneuver my car in order to overtake and escape. Luckier still, I hadn't lost *zanshin* whilst in the traffic queue and was observant enough to notice what was happening before it was too late. *Zanshin* does not mean being on edge all of the time, but is something which should be quietly maintained in the background of our every action. Admittedly, my own personal circumstances in life have heightened my requirement for this attribute somewhat, however; I believe that it is something which can be developed fully under more conventional circumstances through correct training and education.

Self-defense is not about knife disarms, reality drills, or shouting and screaming in each other's faces whilst you practice 'practical' *bunkai*. No, it's about simple modifications to daily routines which lessen the likelihood of you being put in the position of becoming a victim. No self-defense method is failsafe, and a system is only ever as useful as the practitioner it is able to make it. When it comes to self-defense, I wish more people would devote serious effort into understanding how to effectively remove themselves from being involved in a situation, rather than how to end one. Avoidance is always the safest option and without question, the most effective. Any martial art which can successfully teach this can be considered extremely useful and relevant to modern times.

# Listen......Do You Want To Know A Secret?

**Guard posts such as this in Shikinaen were manned by Royal bodyguards who were recruited from the Shuri *bushi***

Anybody with even the slightest interest in *karate* history will be familiar with the popular folklore about how the art was most often taught in remote locations during the middle of the night in order to keep its practice secret and away from prying eyes. This is commonly attributed to the practice of *karate* being outlawed by the occupying Satsuma Samurai, however; there may be another reason.

During the days of the Ryukyu Kingdom a person was highly sought after if they were adept in Chinese language, calligraphy, or martial arts, and skill in any of these areas would enable them to stand a better chance of gaining employment in government offices, providing their family with much needed financial security. The more you excelled in *bujutsu*, the greater chance you stood of becoming a bodyguard or police officer[2]. *Bujutsuka* were also highly respected for their integrity and insight, making them trusted advisors for people in power. For this reason, followers of the martial traditions held their secrets close to their chest for fear of

---

[2] Discussion with Hokama Tetsuhiro sensei, Naha, Okinawa 2011

having their techniques stolen by other practitioners who might then stand a better chance of competing for the same position. For this same reason, students were also chosen very carefully, for you wouldn't want a disciple to be roaming around the Tsuji red light district bragging about the techniques they had learnt at your school, giving away hints to other rivals.

*Bujutsu* in Okinawa around the 19th century was largely confined to the wealthier districts of Shuri, as the areas of Naha and Tomari consisted mainly of merchants who were more concerned with scraping a living than practicing martial arts. Despite this, there was a very small group of martial artists with strong links to China who were active in the Kuninda district of Naha. This group laid the foundations of the art which would later become *Nahadi*. Far from conducting their practice in secret though, the training was in fact quite open, happening throughout the day in an informal manner in the areas of Matsuyama and Naminoue. People would apparently bring along their lunch and whatever training equipment they had at home, and everybody would get together to train and exchange techniques[3]. It must have been quite a sight and the source of much local curiosity, especially for youngsters such as Higashionna Kanryo *sensei* who would eventually go on to study from this same group of masters, led by the famous *Mayaa* Aragaki Seisho.

With the abolishment of the Ryukyu Kingdom the upper classes of Okinawa suddenly found themselves without status or income. It was this more than anything else which forced *karate* to emerge from its self-imposed era of secrecy. The upper class *bujin* now found themselves without the means to provide for their families and this led some to begin teaching martial arts publicly for a fee, thus creating the 'professional *karate* instructor' which has now become so familiar[4].

It should be known however, that despite *karate* now being available to the masses, it was still something which was only pursued by those of a wealthy background who could afford to spend a significant amount of their time on the luxury of training rather than having to scrape a living like everybody else. People at that time had much more important things to worry about rather than wasting their time on *karate*. The situation hasn't changed much I think, all over the world.

Despite *karate* not being very important in the grand scheme of things, skilled practitioners of good character were revered as local heroes, as *bushi*, with their exploits becoming the stuff of legend. Villages would

---

[3] Discussion with Hokama Tetsuhiro, Matsuyama Koen, Okinawa 2011

[4] Discussion with Hokama Tetsuhiro, Nishihara, Okinawa 2011

preserve their stories in song, poetry, theatre and dance in order to entertain, educate and inspire the local population.

*Karate* has never been something for the masses. Yes, it is available to everybody, but it most certainly is not suited to the personal circumstances of everyone. You have to be either very fortunate or particularly strong willed and determined to get your life in order so that you can devote a reasonable amount of time to practice if you wish to develop any real degree of proficiency. Miyazato Eiichi *sensei* advised his followers to arrange their life in order of importance i.e.; family, work, and then *karate*; but many people often use the first two as an excuse for avoiding the third. If the balance between these three areas of life cannot be achieved, perhaps you might be wasting your time?

The Merindo located within the grounds of the Tenpi Jingu in Naminoue educated the youth of Naha in Confucian theories, calligraphy, and Chinese language. The famous *Bubishi* was housed at this location before WW2.

# Go & Ju Eye Methods

Fukuchi sensei's *Go* eyes during *Tensho*

The training of the eyes in *Goju Ryu* is an important area of practice which I feel is slowly being forgotten. There are various exercises contained within *junbi undo* which relate directly to the eyes, but in most cases these are no longer practiced which is a real shame. Richard Barrett *sensei* emphasized various methods of training the eyes at his *dojo*, as does the Hokama *dojo*. Such exercises have their roots in the *Ekkinkyo* and *Senzuikyo*, commonly attributed to the teachings of Daruma.

The *Sanchin* glare is one of the distinguishing features of the *Nahadi* systems, and there is a famous saying attributed to the Uechi tradition which advises the practitioner to develop *'fast hands and tiger eyes'*. Despite this, I was often told off by Yasuda *sensei* of the *Jundokan dojo* for pulling a *'Sanchin* face'. His school of thought was that you should appear perfectly calm and tranquil on the outside, hiding your effort from observers. Although completely lost on me at the time, I think I am beginning to better understand what he was trying to advise me. As well as being a very good *karateka*, Yasuda *sensei* is also a teacher of *Iaido* and Yoga, and his training appeared to be very much focused upon keeping his body healthy and youthful. Anybody who met him was always impressed by the physical feats which he could perform well into his late 70's.

The Naha based traditions still receive a certain amount of negative attention relating to the health problems, high blood pressure and premature deaths which are wrongly attributed to the practice and training methods of *Sanchin*. These silly rumors have never been evidenced and I'm pretty sure that if I sat down and did some maths I would find numerous examples of *Nahadi* practitioners continuing their training well into old age. Yagi *sensei*, Miyazato *sensei*, Yasuda *sensei*, Kinjo *sensei*, Higaonna *sensei*, Aragaki Seisho *sensei*, Toguchi *sensei*, and Higa *sensei* all immediately spring to mind without even having to think too hard. Having said this, if we push ourselves to exhaustion each time we train and we continually abuse our bodies by not practicing in a balanced manner, we will surely cause more harm than good in the long run. I see my training these days as investing for the future, for I want to remain active well into my old age and still able to train and enjoy time with my family.

So, returning to *Go* and *Ju* eye methods.

When training *Sanchin* in accordance with *Go*, the eyes should open wide and glare menacingly, displaying our spirit and animal instinct in order to intimidate and deter the opponent. This is a *Yang* method of using the eyes. The eyes should not focus upon a particular area of the opponent, but should rest on a point which allows you to observe their entire body. I usually look at the area of the throat which allows me to observe any movements of the upper body. Peripheral vision relates directly to the subconscious mind and allows us to react instinctively according to our training. The eyes should be intimidating to look at, and able to make a tiger cower in fear as Funakoshi *sensei* said. I am reminded here about the story of *Bushi* Matsumura defeating his opponent with only his frightening glare! Students of Miyagi *shinshi* also regularly commented upon how intimidating his eyes were during practice. *Sanchin Shime* builds our ability to use the eyes in this manner and allows us to make better use of the Central Nervous System and our primal bodily functions. The essence of using the eyes in a *Go* manner is in projecting the fighting spirit outward and directly into the opponent's soul in order to defeat them mentally.

When training in accordance with *Ju*, the eyes should be used in a more passive manner without projecting energy out of the body. This is a *Yin* method, and is the same way that the eyes are used in the practice of *zazen*. The face should appear passive and calm and the eyes should be half closed and peaceful. In this method the emphasis is upon what is happening within **you** rather than any concerns about the outside world or an external opponent. Miyazato *sensei* made mention of *Sanchin* being moving meditation in his book Okinawa Den Goju Ryu Karate-Do;

*'Zen: there is sitting meditation, standing meditation, lying meditation and moving meditation. Sanchin is moving and standing meditation.'* [5]

Using the eyes in this manner relates to this idea.

Miyazato *sensei* also wrote:

*'Ki is the mysterious power that cannot be seen with the eyes and emanates from the entire body to suppress and overwhelm an opponent.*

*The breath consists of: breathing methods, breathing for life, and breathing to strike an enemy.'* [6]

I believe here that Miyazato *sensei* has provided a very important clue as to how *Sanchin* can be used as both a means of *budo* and *kenko*. It should be noted that the use of the eyes in both circumstances are entirely different and require a completely different mindset.

Within the classical *junbi undo* of *Goju Ryu* there are methods of exercising and developing the eyes by rotating through different planes of movement, by slowly scanning vertical and horizontal objects, by switching between scanning and looking, by contrasting between light and dark using a candle flame, and through massage and immersion in water. Regretfully most of these methods are no longer in regular use.

I will share a couple of traditional exercises here. One method that Richard Barrett *sensei* would use in his *dojo* was to have the room in complete darkness with a single candle in the middle of the room. You would then stare at the candle flame and try not to blink. This was a *Go* method intended to build the ability to zone into a specific detail and extend your intention. It also developed the *'Sanchin* glare', a *Go* attribute intended to overwhelm and intimidate an opponent. Miyagi Chojun *shinshi* also used this same training method and would have the candle standing at head height whilst he was sat in *seiza* in order to strengthen his neck muscles at the same time. Correct posture needs to be maintained throughout in the same way during *Sanchin kata*. This is an example of 'looking' skill.

'Scanning skill' can be developed by staring at a moving object which has a lot of detail, such as a leafy tree swaying in the wind. Whilst observing, you should allow your eyes to take in the entire tree rather than focusing upon a single detail. This is the correct use of the eyes when engaging an opponent. Switching between 'scanning skill' and 'looking skill' becomes important when it comes to attacking specific targets. This method can

---

[5] Okinawa Den Goju Ryu Karate-Do, Miyazato, p68

[6] Okinawa Den Goju Ryu Karate-Do, Miyazato, p68

be practiced by using 'scanning skill' to look at the entire picture and then instantly switch to 'looking skill' to pierce a specific detail such as a single leaf.

It is said that the *Qi* follows intention and intention is led by the eyes. This is an important clue when it comes to understanding the reason for turning the head during the turns in *Sanchin kata*. When striking a specific target or vital area, the eyes switch from 'scanning' to 'looking' and intention is placed into that particular vital point through the striking tool in order to strike a decisive blow. This can be considered the way of switching the eyes from *Ju* to *Go*. *Ju* possesses calmness, fluidity, instinctive reaction and conserving energy. *Go* displays assertiveness, determination and extends energy out of the body and into the target. An understanding of the correct use of both methods is essential in *bujutsu*.

**Kannon's expression typifies *Ju***

# **Could You Learn From This Teacher?**

There are many different parts to *karate* and this can be very convenient for people who wish to treat the art like an all-you-can-eat buffet. With so many different dishes to choose from, you can take lots from the ones you like whilst avoiding the dishes that don't suit your tastes so well.

It is quite different though when you are invited into somebody's home for dinner. When presented with a meal there may well be things on the plate that you don't like, however; it would be considered bad manners to leave them aside without first trying them or to openly show your dislike, for your host will have put much effort into preparing that meal for you to enjoy. To hurt their feelings and repay their kindness with bad manners would be very rude.

True *karatedo* is like the latter example. There will be parts of the training and the underlying philosophy that you dislike or don't agree with (usually because you want to behave one way but are expected to act another). Either you accept and get on with it, or you spend your time avoiding the things which do not suit you, pretending to yourself and everyone around you that you're still embracing the full art. This would be like hiding the parts of the meal you dislike in the plant pots or feeding them to the family pet under the table so that the host doesn't notice.

*Karatedo* carries with it an underlying philosophy and moral code. It may come as some surprise but THIS is the important bit! Not the punches, kicks, belts, trophies or fame and recognition. It is this same aim that proves to be the most challenging part of training because it means you can have no excuses for not doing it. The behavior of a *karateka* (which incidentally is identical to the behavior of any good person) is very black and white. It is either right, or it is wrong. There is no space for grey, no room for excuses.

Kato *sensei* (my new made up fictional celebrity *karate* teacher) is a phenomenal athlete. His physical abilities are second to none. He has applications for *kata* which are brutally effective, and has an impeccable lineage which can be traced directly back to the founder of the style. He runs a well-equipped *dojo* and receives many visitors from all over the world. He is a regular contributor to magazines and has produced a number of books. To top it all off, he is an excellent teacher and has successfully trained a number of students to be able to replicate his awesome physical abilities.

Kato *sensei* though, displays a very different persona outside of the *dojo*. For all his talk about the various positive character traits which can be gained through the study of *karate*, he often acts in a vulgar manner. He hits on the wives of his students. He has had a number of affairs behind his own wife's back. He regularly uses illegal drugs, and has been arrested for a drunken brawl in the street, which he instigated by the way.

Inside the *dojo* though he is an attentive and considerate teacher, very kind to his students and always brings the best out in them.

Would you continue to learn under such a person if you knew their background?

If you did, how would you feel about yourself?

If you respected this man greatly before knowing all of this, would you jump to his defense upon hearing these things without taking the time to investigate why this information had suddenly surfaced?

In the movie The Karate Kid (the original one, not the one where they all do *kung fu*???), Mr Miyagi says to Daniel san *"either karate you do yes, or karate you do no. You karate do 'guess so', sooner or later squish, just like grape"*.

Never a truer word said.

Wherever there is a marked contrast between what a teacher says and what they do, there is a sure sign that they have little understanding of the art they are supposedly passing on. The sad thing is, the general attitude of the majority of people practicing these days appears to be one of 'hey, we're all human' and in more worrying cases such things are even openly admired. As I have mentioned on numerous occasions before, there is very little which separates *karate* from any other martial art when it comes to the physical techniques. What does define *karatedo* though is the ongoing pursuit of positive character traits by the individuals who are engaged in its true practice. The reason this part is not very popular is that this is **THE** most difficult part of training and you will no doubt fail many more times than you succeed in the early stages. Confronting yourself honestly when it comes to character flaws and then tackling them with strong determination requires letting go of the ego and a willingness to admit to yourself that you still have a long way left to go. It requires you to stop making excuses for yourself and once this part is achieved, it allows you to see through the excuses of others. This is not passing judgment; it is simply learning the skill of perception and being able to distinguish excuses from reasons. Going through this process of self discovery is what creates the *sensei*. Judging from the behavior of many people holding powerful positions within the *karate* world, I wonder whether there are many real *sensei* left these days?

# **Take Care Of Your Health**

Our health is something which many of us take for granted, that is until something goes wrong which forces us stand up and take notice. As *karateka* we spend hours polishing and refining our techniques, sharpening our impact tools and forging our spirit, but on how many occasions is this combined with a poor diet, excessive drinking, smoking, or an otherwise unhealthy lifestyle?

Without our health we cannot do anything, so should this not be our number one priority above all else? In the military great care is taken over the cleanliness of a soldier's uniform, eating utensils, living quarters and of course, the condition of their weapon. Whilst this serves to instill certain qualities in the soldier, it also ensures that when they are deployed in the field, good habits are ingrained which help prevent the onset of disease, keeping the soldier healthy and able to fight more effectively. If the soldier is unable to fight due to illness caused through poor drills, he is useless to his colleagues. This is the same with *karate*. If we become unable to practice due to lifestyle choices which have an adverse effect upon our health, exactly what do we hope to gain from our training? True, the body may be only a vehicle which carries the spirit; however, if that vehicle is falling apart, how confident are we that we will reach our destination?

My *sensei's* wife runs a health food shop in the town where they live. They often get people inside the shop browsing the various items and sometimes asking questions about what products might be good for their particular circumstances. One day a lady came in to enquire about Cod Liver Oil as she was suffering from painful joints and a general lack of mobility. My *sensei's* wife offered her a good quality oil which was perfect for her condition, informing her of the various benefits. The lady was really interested and asked for the price. *Sensei's* wife told her, and upon hearing this, the lady said it was far too expensive and then left the shop. A couple of days later, the same lady returned to the shop to show off her new hairstyle which she proudly boasted had cost her a small fortune.

I find this story really funny! The lady obviously wasn't willing to spend much money on the inside of her body, but on the outside which everybody else could see, she was willing to spend a lot. It is the same with famous celebrities who get lots of cosmetic surgery and then go out partying all night and taking drugs. They might have attractive young looking bodies on the outside, but inside they probably have the internal organs of an 80 year old!

Perhaps if you could wear your liver on the outside of your body so that everybody could see it, people would be getting cosmetic surgery to ensure it was a nice healthy looking color? You could even get designer labels sewn onto it!

Taira Masaji *sensei* of the *jundokan* once told me something interesting about his approach to *hojo undo*. He said that *hojo undo* conditions the inside of the body so that it is not damaged by *karate* training. His own particular manner of generating force is physically demanding and can be described as an explosion which occurs in the *tanden*, combined with forceful breathing. He said that the body must be sufficiently conditioned through *hojo undo* to not be harmed by his method. I was particularly impressed by this balance of *Go* and *Ju* in his personal approach, and wondered

why this theory is not nearly as popular as his applications? Again, I think it comes down to wanting to show off something on the outside for other people to see rather than wanting to feel a benefit on the inside which is known only to you.

In *karate* there are very different reasons for why we all practice. Some train purely for recreation. Some for self-defense or the opportunity to compete. Others for the health benefits. From my experience I would say that there are more practitioners in Okinawa who choose to practice *karate* simply because they think it is good for their health, and this is also one of my main reasons for training. Having seen many practitioners over the age of 70 still training regularly and enjoying it, *karate* fills me with the hope that I might be able to stay physically active long into my twilight years while everybody else is taking it easy. However, I also know that *karate* cannot achieve this alone and that I must make a conscious effort to nurture the inside of my body through a good diet, exercise and lifestyle, as well as the outside through hard, sensible training.

# Osoji

**Richard Barrett *sensei's* Shinsokan *dojo***

As each year draws to a close at my *dojo* we begin to prepare for the year ahead by reflecting upon our successes and failures of the previous 12 months. A major part of this is the act of *Osoji*.

*Soji* (cleaning) is performed by the members of my *dojo* before and after every training session, but *Osoji* is a little different and is conducted during our *Hatsu Geiko* (1st training session after New Year). All of the members assist with cleaning everything top to bottom, inside and out. This act ensures that the *dojo* is free of any dirt from the previous year so that we are ready to start afresh. The same ritual is conducted in the spirits of the *karateka*, and is an act of ridding ourselves of baggage and clutter which might interfere with our future practice. The most important part of *Osoji* is learning how to let go of the unnecessary.

One exception to *soji* is made in that the various *hojo undo* tools are not cleaned. Come to think of it, they are never cleaned. The *hojo undo* implements should be cleaned through use, meaning that no dust is allowed to settle. If ever you see a *dojo* with dusty equipment, this is probably a good indication that they are seldom used, and this may indicate lazy students or more likely a lazy teacher!

Everything inside a *dojo* must serve a purpose, or else it is just taking up space (and this includes students!). The photos, the *kanji*, the equipment, the trophies and certificates (just kidding!), all must serve to teach a lesson and assist us with our training, or else they are just decoration and belong in a museum.

Much has been said on various martial arts blogs and discussion forums about the need for a *dojo kun*. The impression I get is that it is not often viewed as an important part of most people's *karate* anymore. Many people said that they have a *dojo kun* hanging in their *dojo*, but it is never actively studied by the *dojo* members. If this is the case then it would be best to get rid of it altogether as it is just taking up wall space. This would be like having a *chiishi* in the *dojo* but not knowing how to use it. If ever a visitor came to the *dojo* and asked about that *chiishi*, it would cause great embarrassment if we had to admit it was only there for decoration and we had no idea what it was for.

The end of a year is also always a new beginning. This offers the perfect chance for a little reflection and soul searching. Perhaps a good question for all of us would be;

Why do you practice, and what are you trying to achieve from your training?

The answers to these questions may well indicate which parts of your training are essential or non-essential. Just be careful that through trimming off the non-essential you do not lose the essence of *karate* and turn it into something quite different altogether.

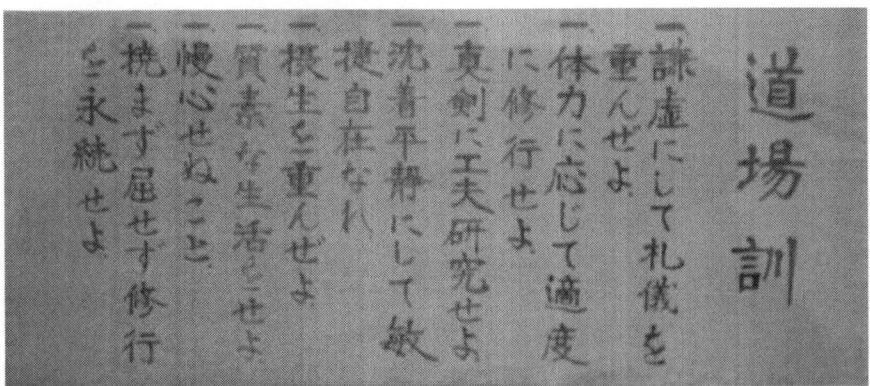

**Dojo Kun at the Jundokan**

# **Letting Go**

This is a tricky subject, one that has plagued the minds of martial artists for many centuries, yet despite great advances in technology and the improved understanding of how our minds work, we seem to have made little progress in discovering how to overcome this problem.

It is sometimes said that 1 hours training in the morning is equivalent to 3 hours in the evening. Perhaps this has something to do with our state of mind in the morning which is generally calmer and yet to be tarnished by the happenings of that day? You see, throughout the day we inevitably collect clutter. The more clutter we collect, the more difficult it becomes to settle our minds and concentrate fully upon a single task. This clutter seemingly attracts even more clutter and can be triggered by a minor thing such as the train to work being delayed which subsequently makes you late for an important meeting. Because of this you get shouted at by your boss. You then work extra hard during the day, skipping lunch. With eyes straining at a computer screen and no rest or fuel for the body you become irritable, you then take into the journey home, which just so happens to be an overcrowded train during the hot summer weather. Somebody steps on your toe and you curse at them under your breath. Arriving home, your partner notices you are in a bad mood and so avoids you. You leave for training, arrive at the *dojo*, and then you have to empty the mind of all these things in order to concentrate upon an instant. Ok, this is a particularly bad day I'm describing here, but hopefully it demonstrates the kind of clutter we can collect and carry around with us.

In *budo* we have the expression *'ichi go, ichi e'* which means 'one encounter, one opportunity'. This suggests that we should endeavor to dedicate ourselves fully to a single instant, both physically and mentally. There are a number of rituals preserved in all classical *budo dojo* which can assist a person in ridding themselves of daily clutter, the first of which is performing *rei* upon entering the *dojo*. Following this you will change into your practice wear. There is then *soji* to be performed. The lesson usually then begins with a period of *mokuso*. A further series of *rei* will then be performed toward the *shomen* wall, the *sensei*, and to the other students present. At the beginning of an exercise, we will then perform a further *rei* before adopting *yoi kamae*. I've probably missed further examples, but from the top of my head this is 7 separate opportunities to clear your mind and commit to the moment, all before a 'martial' movement has even been performed. These are not empty rituals designed to preserve cultural traits or to play act at being *'bushi'*, these are valuable learning experiences to be grasped greedily at every opportunity. If our mind remains 'caught' elsewhere, we will be unable to respond instinctively and decisively.

During the course of a typical lesson we will inevitably make many mistakes, which may be drawn to our attention by our *sensei*. Of course, such corrections should be committed to memory and absorbed, but don't allow the mind to stick on this point, impeding the rest of your movements. This is particularly evident in *kata* where a mistake early on in the performance can cause the remainder to quickly go to ruin. When an error is made it is important to first acknowledge it and then immediately move on as though it never happened. In application we do not have the luxury of feeling sorry for ourselves or allowing our spirit to drop because we made a mistake. No, we must work twice as hard to compensate for that error and regain the initiative. The same applies to mistakes in daily life. Dwelling on them for too long achieves nothing, take action to achieve a positive outcome. This is not to say that *budoka* should not feel emotion. This would be quite ridiculous! We are human beings and it is ok to feel sad, angry, excitable, scared, etc. The only difference is that we should acknowledge that we are feeling such emotions, but not allow our conduct to be ruled by them. I remember a great phrase used by Dave Lowry about a time he lost his temper during *kenjutsu* practice and his *sensei* scolded him saying 'anger is a luxury you cannot afford'. I find it really worthwhile to think about the wisdom behind this phrase.

*Be calm in mind and swift in action......* As somebody with a particularly stressful working environment, I have thought about these subjects often, and this has led me to adopting a few practices which I have shamelessly stolen from various sources. One of my favorites which I will share with you comes from my brother in law. He is a keen surfer, and it is in this environment that his soul is most peaceful. As an accountant with a huge workload, he can at times feel a bit overwhelmed at work. In order to settle his thoughts and calm his mind he keeps a pot of surfboard wax on his desk which he smells whenever things start to get on top of him. That particular scent always takes him back to the environment where he is happiest, and helps him to once again concentrate on the task at hand. I've found this to be a great technique, you just have to discover what smells or sounds work for you.

Whilst on the subject of 'catching' and 'letting go', I find it interesting that during the practice of *kakie*, many of us seem to share a common problem of being overly concerned with keeping hold of a limb after we have grabbed it. For example we might attempt a joint lock which is then successfully defended, but rather than quickly disengaging and responding with strikes, the tendency seems to be to want to keep hold of that limb for dear life, almost like a safety blanket. Looking into this further it seems that human beings have a grab reflex which instinctively makes them want to keep hold. I personally have found this reflex very difficult to overcome, and it's interesting how much this corresponds to life in general.

*Kakie* practice with Richard Barrett *sensei*

# Two Big Diseases

**Two figures showing postures similar to those found within the Bubishi**

Studying *karatedo* is very dangerous. No, I'm not talking about the ability to fell an opponent with a single strike, or being able to rip flesh from a living goat; I'm speaking of a much more basic thing, keeping on the right track. For people at the beginning of their journey this is pretty easy because the teacher says and you do. It is as simple as that. For more advanced students though, who are now taking responsibility for their own training and research whilst still hopefully under the guidance of a good sensei, there is a real danger that you can stray so far from the path that you might end up practicing something quite different to what you think. *Goju Ryu Karate* practice is very easy. What I mean by this is there is a very small syllabus consisting of *junbi undo, hojo undo, kata*, and 2-person training drills when you have the luxury of having a partner. This is all that is needed, period!

Despite being very easy in this regard, *karate* is also very difficult for many people who may feel stifled, bored, or stripped of the opportunity to develop, add to, and put their own mark on the art. This of course has led to many offshoots and the whole jumbled mess which is collectively referred to as *karate* these days, although most of us are practicing very different things with completely different aims. There are, in my opinion, two big diseases in *karate*. Boredom and the ego. Boredom will lead people to start looking elsewhere in order to 'add' the things which they think are missing from the art. Cross training is a good thing, but it depends upon the reasons for doing so. To train with other people in an effort to better understand 'why' you do things a certain way is extremely beneficial, and this will often open up many new avenues for you to research in your own practice. Over time though, you will hopefully discover that there is nothing new under the sun and every art is applying the same principles from a slightly different approach. *'Many paths lead up the mountain, but there is only one moon to be seen by those who reach the summit.'* The danger of too much cross training without purpose is that you can become a 'collector'. In Okinawa such people were referred to as *'Hachindi'* which had the negative connotation of being a master of remembering techniques and making money.

Sometimes I wonder if my 24 hour day is somehow shorter than everybody else's. As I have said before, my own personal training consists of nothing more than *junbi undo*, *kata*, and *hojo undo*. I occasionally practice a little *kobudo kata*, but this is not a serious study on my part, more a luxury to enjoy the movements and shared history. If I ever win the lottery perhaps I can spend more time training so that I can improve my *kobudo* and study it properly. For now though, I am lucky enough to have a job which allows me time to train. I also have a *dojo* at my house where I will spend some more time practicing every day. Despite these fortunate circumstances, I still do not have enough time to study everything, and at times I feel like a 'plate spinner' trying to balance many areas of my practice to prevent one of them from falling! I wonder how some people have the time to add *kata* from other styles, 2-person training drills picked up from here and there, grappling systems, weapons systems, studying multiple arts, etc... How much is understood of all these different things? How well are they integrated to work with each other so as not to cause conflict of interests when it comes to responding instinctively? How well suited are the individual delivery systems of each art so as not to interfere with each other? Such things are not to be taken lightly for a split seconds hesitation when it comes to responding can mean the difference between escaping safely or becoming a victim. It depends on your reasons for training though I guess....

The boredom issue can prove too much for many to overcome and this is why very few students stick around for long enough to learn any more than a surface level of physical techniques. Before an understanding is developed, they are already off looking elsewhere for the things that are 'missing' from their school. The photograph at the beginning of this article was taken at the entrance of Fukushuen in Kume Naha. You can see two figures performing postures from the *bubishi*. I have visited these gardens more times than I can remember over the past 10 years, but never once had I noticed these figures until they were pointed out to me last year. They were hidden in plain view all along! This continues to be the case with my study of *Goju Ryu*. Almost every time I train I am rewarded with another little insight into the character of a technique, a slightly different method of applying it in a slightly different context. To every question which has ever arisen from *kakie* training and 'real life' (I hate that term!) encounters, *kata* has held the answers, every time. It just sometimes takes a particular set of circumstances to create the right questions. It takes a lot of faith to continue training with patience, knowing that immediate rewards are few and a lifetime of dedication is required. I can understand why this might be too much of an obligation for many, particularly in today's society where quick results are both promised and expected. *Goju Ryu* is quite stubborn and will only give you in return what you are first willing to offer as an investment.

The second big disease is the ego. This is what happens when people want to put their own mark on something in order to become wealthy, successful or famous in varying measures depending on the person. I am aware that this article is already sounding very 'pointing the finger' in its manner, so I want to assure you that I too have been guilty of many of these things I mentioned in the past. I've just been lucky enough to have the diseases treated in their early stages whilst they could still be cured. This again comes down to having a good *sensei*.

The ego will lead a teacher to become an entertainer, sacrificing what they initially believed to be true in order to keep students or please the crowd, whatever that crowd may be. This is either financially motivated or due to a need for constant encouragement and acknowledgement from others to boost their own self-importance. This has led to the phenomenon of the *karate* celebrity. Such people can be flown into your country, first class of course, then put up at a 5 star hotel with all expenses paid, picked up each day by limousine and then taken to a huge hall full of hundreds of students eager to collectively train under them all for the promise of a quick rushed photograph at the end. After 'training' everyone can then have a beer together and socialize, perhaps even grease a few palms, slap a few backs, and secure that all important next rank promotion. If you want to go train in Okinawa, perhaps such a celebrity might offer to write you a letter of introduction for a fee, otherwise of course such an opportunity is not available for 'regular people'. Usually you see, you cannot even get to meet such great masters, let alone train with them. Yeah, right.......

The challenge of *Goju Ryu Karatedo* is simply this; continue your training with patience.....

Nothing more is needed in *Goju Ryu*, it's already there. We are lucky enough to follow a tradition where great care has been taken to ensure that you have all the tools you need in order to develop an understanding of the art. All you have to do is train. Don't be in too much of a rush. Don't re-invent the wheel, and it clearly isn't broken so please stop trying to fix it. Add to this list sticking to what you believe to be true, not getting too full of your own self-importance, and not being afraid to take responsibility for yourself without having to rely upon others, and you have a challenge which **will** last a lifetime.

Good luck!

*Suparinpei* **practice on a quiet beach**

# Teaching Methods

**Group *kata* practice at the Jundokan**

I think that the order in which the *kata* are presented in *Goju Ryu* is actually quite insignificant and I disagree with the way some groups dictate that you cannot learn certain *kata* until you reach a particular grade. In my opinion this is only done in order to promote a hierarchy, generate revenue, keep the student in their place, and encourages a 'one size fits all' type of *karate* which is only beneficial to large groups. To say that you cannot learn *Suparinpei* until you are *yondan* or above is quite absurd and causes an unnecessary delay in committing the sequence to memory, as well as introducing this physically demanding *kata* at a time where the student is most likely already past their peak physical condition, making things more difficult for them in the long run. Challenging techniques such as the *furi geri* require many years of practice, and this is best done at the earliest suitable opportunity so that the student has more time to perfect it. Some students of Miyagi Chojun *sensei* such as Yagi Meitoku *sensei* learnt *Suparinpei* immediately after *Sanchin* which would indicate that Miyagi *sensei* felt it appropriate to introduce the *kata* at a relatively early stage of a student's development.

In our group students are encouraged to commit each *kata* to memory as soon as they are able so that we can then move past the 'memory test' stage of training. Whilst a student remains inside this memory test period, the techniques of *kata* are unnatural and remain difficult to apply. Fighting applications do not occur readily, and the *kata* do not appear very useful in real situations at this stage. Once a student is able to perform the *kata* without having to think about which move comes next, or whether their arm is in the right position; they can then devote their attention to visualizing an opponent and adding the required intent to the movements. *Kata* then becomes an extremely useful tool, removing the need to always have a training partner in order to practice the various fighting techniques contained within a system.

Regarding the order of teaching *kata*, of course *Sanchin* must come first. *Gekisai* then helps to introduce certain ideas which can assist the novice when it comes to learning the classical *kata*, but after this, who is to say that *seipai* is any more advanced than *saifa*, or more important? In my opinion, the order of the *kata* is no more significant than the order in which songs are presented on a music album. All of the songs are different and have a certain 'feeling' attached to them, and owing to this, each person might have a different favorite song and play this more often than the other tracks. The 'order' of the tracks just makes for easier listening and helps to create a nice blend of fast and slow songs, serious and light hearted songs. You get the idea?

Perhaps you would enjoy the music so much that you learnt to play it on the guitar. You might have a few friends who also play instruments, so when you meet up you can all play together. Of course when you are all together it is important to be playing the same song otherwise it would sound awful! This is similar to what happens in group training. When *karate* was originally taught it was done in back yards, living rooms or graveyards; there were no 'group' classes. Each person was taught according to their individual needs, physiques and personality traits, and this worked very well until suddenly *karate* was being taught under very different circumstances. Teachers were now facing groups of 30+ students rather than 2 or 3. How can you teach such a large group? Luckily somebody figured out that in the military they use drill to get everybody moving together as a combined unit. The days of teaching 2 or 3 people are for the large part gone, and to be perfectly honest, I would not know where to begin with teaching such a large group. I would have absolutely nothing to offer and so would probably resort to 'drill', marching up and down doing *kihon* and counting *'ichi, ni, san'*. Perhaps everybody could also perform *kata* together as a group, with me counting *'ichi, ni, san'*. Now, I am not pointing the finger here, ranting that everybody else is doing it all wrong, no, I am just saying that I do not know how to teach large groups of people due to the particular circumstances in which I have learnt *karate*. My teaching methods would be very inadequate and leave most people bored, wasting their time for most of the lesson. Due to the circumstances of my life, and my own personal beliefs about what *karate* is, or should be, I teach in a very small space to a very, very small group of people. I find myself in some ways, in a similar situation to the *karate* teachers at the turn of the 20th century who were trying to pass on an art to a population who were pretty much disinterested in it. Make no mistake; before Itosu *sensei* revamped the old custom of secrecy and private teaching, *karate* was in grave danger of becoming extinct. If not for him, I doubt any of us would be practicing today.

My lessons are very boring. Each time we begin with *junbi undo*, and following this we will practice *Sanchin*. Whichever weak point catches my eye the most for each student then determines what happens for the remainder of the lesson. According to each person's main fault I will 'guide' toward a particular *hojo undo* implement and certain exercises in order to instill a certain feeling or correct some structural fault. In addition to this there will also be basic *sandan gi* and *kakie*. This for me contains the essence of *Goju Ryu*. If there is still time, I will advise upon one particular *kata* for each student. There is rarely any order to this. Again, depending upon what I see in each person's *kata* I might point toward a certain *hojo undo* exercise, or show a certain variation of *oyo* to generate some thought. I rarely teach each person the same application and I most certainly do not know the 'original' *bunkai* of any techniques. I think most people would become very bored at my *dojo*, in fact I know this to be true because most people leave within a year of entering. This has always been the case though, even with students of the great Higashionna Kanryo *sensei* who could tolerate not only the challenging physical training, but also the boredom of having a *Sanchin* based martial art. This is true not only of Okinawan *Goju Ryu*, but of any method which has a form of *Sanchin* at its core.

At my *dojo* everybody is different with their own particular strengths and weaknesses. For me to teach everybody the same thing in the same way would in my opinion, be unfair to them. I would be forcing them to fit inside a box which perhaps was not suited to contain them. *Goju Ryu* can be applied by anyone; male or female, strong or weak, but in order for it to be effective it must be taught according to the person's individual needs. Miyagi Chojun *sensei* himself did this.

*Kata* are the textbooks. These are supposed to be studied by everybody and so must remain intact so that our own individual habits and traits do not make it more difficult for the next person in the chain to learn. Once something is changed, something is lost. What works for you might not work for your student, so we should try our best to preserve the *kata* unchanged. This way, everybody has an equal opportunity to study.

I'm in danger of veering off subject here, so getting back to the original point; both methods of teaching have their own strengths and weaknesses. In order to preserve and promote *karate*, it has to be taught and passed on to the next generation. For this reason large group classes are a good thing. For the essence to be grasped though, an individual approach is more beneficial I think.

Everybody is unique and learns in different ways. How can you help a student to catch an idea? What training methods can you recommend to them? This is one of the things I enjoy most about sharing my *dojo* with others. Perhaps all we can do is teach according to what we believe in our heart to be the correct way? It all comes down to what you want your *karate* to be.

# More On Miyagi Sensei's Self Defence Methods

**Miyagi Chojun shinshi**

My wife and I were talking over lunch one day when she told me about a dream that she had during the previous night. The dream concerned two burglars breaking into our house at night whilst I was away, and my wife found herself confronted by them in the kitchen whilst our little boy was sleeping upstairs in his room. In the dream, my wife had her phone in her hand during the confrontation which she used to throw into the face of one of the burglars in order to create a distraction. Then she woke from the dream. I was laughing while she told me this, but I was also very impressed at the choice of tactics from her subconscious mind (although I would have preferred it if she had called the police on her phone before throwing it at the burglars!).

The story reminded me of a conversation I had with Yasuda Tetsunosuke *sensei* of the *Jundokan* over lunch some years ago. Yasuda *sensei* mentioned how during the years following WW2, Miyagi *sensei* would always ensure that he carried some small change in case he were to fall victim to robbers. In the first instance he would try to talk his way out of trouble, using the small change to hand over to the robber, conceding defeat and avoiding the need for fighting. If however the situation was more serious or the robber was armed with a weapon, Miyagi *sensei* would use the coins to throw into the face of his attacker to create a distraction. I do not know if Miyagi *sensei* ever had the misfortune to try out his idea?

This story created such an impression on me that I continue to use this method to this day. As part of my job, I sometimes have to go into dangerous neighborhoods alone in order to gather intelligence whilst trying to blend in with the locals. When I do this I keep some coins in my hand, ready immediately to throw into the face of an opponent so that I can escape. To give you an idea of the effectiveness of this method, I once saw a man get hit with a one pound coin in the mouth and it knocked his front teeth out onto the floor in front of him. I have also had coins thrown at me on many occasions during public disorder, and it is very unnerving, even whilst wearing protective equipment. When thrown at speed, it is almost impossible to see the projectile, and so it is very difficult to avoid being hit. If a coin were to hit the attacker in the eye, I'm sure it would provide ample time to escape.

Although *karate* is said to be a martial art for gentlemen (*kunshi no budo*), it is also the art of the intelligent man. Being intelligent about self-defense means avoiding troublesome spots, but if circumstances mean you must be present in such locations, be prepared and be ready so that you are not caught on the back foot.

Although Miyagi *sensei* was rumored to be the strongest *karateka* of his generation, it is interesting to see that his overall strategy when it came to fighting was to either lose face by conceding defeat, or 'cheat' in order to escape. As *karateka*, perhaps we should concentrate on finding more ways to cheat in order to protect ourselves?

# The Dojo

**The Karate Kenkyukai dojo**

Each year our group conducts an endurance challenge based around *hojo undo* to raise money for various charities. These challenges always involve a high number of repetitions of different exercises and take many hours to complete. After enduring such a challenge, one of my students commented that they had never really taken so much notice of the various photographs and *shodo* (calligraphy) which are hanging on the walls of the *dojo* until they experienced the challenge. When you have nothing else to concentrate upon during a large number of repetitions, such things become much more interesting I suppose; anything to take the mind away from the discomfort.

Everything within the *dojo* needs to have a purpose. That is to say, everything should help teach the student something. If a photograph is there just for decoration, maybe showing a past achievement or a younger, fitter, better looking you; perhaps that photograph should be taken down and replaced with something more beneficial.

In my own *dojo*, all of the photographs are historical and help tell the tale of *Goju Ryu's* development from the days of Higashionna Kanryo *sensei*, up until the later part of Miyagi Chojun *sensei's* life. I have also been careful to choose photographs which I can refer to regarding certain technical aspects which I want to draw a student's attention to as a visual aid.

The *shodo* too are important as they help to provide a balance in the education of a student. Much of what happens in the *dojo* relates directly to the physical, so it is good for a student to be able to see these different *shodo* at times when they are cleaning the *dojo*, giving them a chance to reflect upon their meaning and what place they might have within their own lives. This addresses *bun bu ryo do*, the combined path of martial and academic studies.

I do not force students to learn the meanings of the *shodo*, the names of the people in the photographs, or specific dates concerning the history of *Goju Ryu*, however; it would be very embarrassing for them if ever there was a visitor who asked a question relating to something in the *dojo* to which they had to reply 'I don't know'. The responsibility is upon them to ensure they don't let themselves down. Barrett *sensei* used to have a *shodo* in his *dojo* which said 'to ask is but a moments shame, but to remain ignorant is a lifelong shame'. In other words, if you don't know something, find out!

If you are a student in a *dojo* which has some of the things I have mentioned above, take the time to make sure you know what everything is, and why it's there. It is your *dojo*, so take some pride in knowing everything about it.

A few years back I was at a world famous *dojo* in Okinawa which has a number of beautiful *shodo* on almost every wall, including a large scroll which was handwritten by Miyagi Chojun *sensei*. I'm unable to read Japanese so I asked one of my seniors about the meaning of the scroll. He said he didn't know. I asked about 5 different people during my stay, and not one of them knew. What a shame. Luckily part of this scroll has been translated in Hokama Tetsuhiro *sensei's* excellent book History and Traditions of Okinawan Karate as follows;

*'What is karate? You don't carry a weapon. Its use during times of peace is to train the spirit as well as the body. This will bring you good health and a long life. In an emergency you can respond without hesitation.'* - Miyagi Chojun sensei.

The same is also true of the equipment in a *dojo*. If it's there, use it! If time is not allocated during a lesson, perhaps your *sensei* might allow you to arrive early so that you can hit the *machiwara* before training, or use some of the *hojo undo* equipment. I'm sure they would be impressed with your enthusiasm. Again, know the use and history of the equipment and if you don't know, find out!

There is a certain something about a 'real' *dojo* which is very hard to put your finger on. As you enter inside, the air feels alive. Such an atmosphere is created by thousands of combined hours of sweat from the many people who have stomped their way across the floor in attempt to polish their technique and spirit. The air seems to reverberate from *machiwara* strikes which were already confined to the past from the moment they struck the target. An empty *dojo* is a very special place to be....

I have been very lucky throughout my life because I have almost always trained in a 'traditional' *dojo*. Of course I have also trained in many church halls, community centers and sports halls too. I don't think such places can compare, and I mean no disrespect when I say this, for I know that many people are doing the best they can.

The *dojo* is a relatively new addition to *karate*, but in my opinion, it is a very welcome one. Barrett *sensei* once asked me 'is it possible to really learn *Goju Ryu* without a *dojo*?'

My answer, in short; No.

'But they used to train in back gardens in their underwear!' I hear you say! Yes I know, however; look around the surrounding area in these photographs. There is training equipment everywhere. To really learn *Goju Ryu* you must hit things and you must lift things. This is a major difference between conveniently having everything to hand at a *dojo*, as opposed to having to make do at a hired hall which is shared by other people. If a technique feels weak or incorrect, go hit that or do this exercise until you get the right feeling. This is the major benefit of a *dojo*.

I don't think *Goju Ryu* can be learnt without *hojo undo*, and I think in order to give *hojo undo* the importance it deserves, the tools need to be within reach at all times, not locked away in a cupboard only to be dragged out for a quick 15 minutes during the lesson.

If you don't have a *dojo*, how can you make this happen for yourself? Build the tools, have them at home, and use them! Every serious practitioner can turn their garden into a *dojo* without inconveniencing everyone else in the family. The tools are small and take up very little space. Your real training should be done at home anyway, so make your training be what you want it to be rather than wishing it was something else. Two of my students have built their own *dojo* out of nothing more than a garden shed containing a *machiwara* and various *hojo undo* implements. They have also taken care to give it that authentic feel by having an *ishi ganto* at the entrance which I bought for them in Okinawa and a couple of *Shisa*. Unperturbed by the relative lack of space or their individual circumstances, they took the opportunity to create for themselves a space where they can practice a little every day. This is very admirable and they will become better *karateka* for it.

The ancient *dojo* of the Tomari *Bushi*

# **Be polite!!!!**

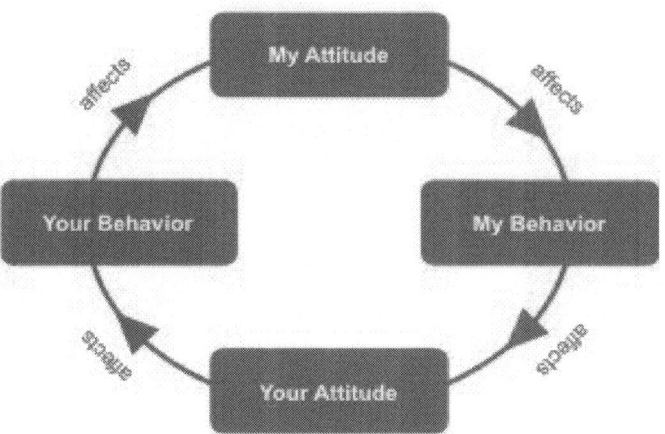

Figure 1: The Betari Box

A friend of mine was getting ready for his first visit to Okinawa and he asked if I had any books which explained the correct etiquette for how to behave in the *dojo* which might assist him during his stay. I replied that I thought he would be fine, as he has a good teacher.

You see, my friend is not blessed with natural traits which make him stand out as an athlete, but what he has in huge quantities is politeness, humility and heart. These traits alone will make him a welcome visitor to any *dojo* which he chooses to visit, of this I am quite sure.

For anybody yet to visit and train in Okinawa, or at any classical *dojo* around the world, there are certain protocols which must be followed if you expect to receive any help. If you are perceived as being rude, you will simply be ignored. You will most likely not be shouted at, or kicked out of the *dojo* (unless you are exceptionally offensive!), but you will definitely be treated with complete indifference and left to you own devices. If when training, your seniors are constantly on your back, correcting and scrutinizing your every move; this is probably a good indication that you are well thought of and are considered worthy of their assistance.

Like it or not, this is *budo* and this is life.

I find it mildly amusing to watch people using rudeness as a tool to get their own way. When a mistake is made by a waiter at a restaurant for example, rather than politely and quietly bringing it to the attention of the waiter, the customer might complain loudly and make demands. They create a big scene and embarrass themselves by causing everybody else in the room to look at them. They single themselves out for attention, and this is exactly what we try not to do in *karate*. This is self-defense. If you are asking something of another person, be polite. The other person will be much more forthcoming and willing to engage with you, rather than thinking you are rude and simply ignoring you.

The Betari Box is an excellent example of the thought and behavior processes which occur as a result of how we communicate with each other.

When I am working I will always approach people with politeness. Their response will dictate how the rest of the encounter unfolds. Some people respond in kind with politeness, and the encounter finishes without incident and me thinking 'what a nice guy'. Many people though respond with hostility immediately, which then begins a negative cycle. This principle can be applied to all situations where we have an interaction with another person.

It is important to understand this from a self-defense point of view. If we effectively use communication and swallow our ego, most times we will be able to avoid conflict. This does not apply to ambush type attacks where a person is intent upon making you a victim of course.

How does *karate* teach this? Through use of the *dojo kun*. Who would have thought the *dojo kun* could relate to fighting?

If we remember to 'be humble and polite' when dealing with people, if we 'live a plain life' so as not to attract unwanted attention, if we remain 'calm in mind and swift in action' in order to escape an escalating situation, if we 'take care of our health' to make sure we carry no injuries into a potentially dangerous scenario, and have the fitness to run away and escape (there's that word again!). If we can avoid being 'too proud of ourselves' and have the strength of character to walk away from a situation in front of people who might perceive us as being weak or cowardly, then yes, the *dojo kun* can have everything to do with fighting, or perhaps more accurately how to avoid it. More than this, it teaches how to avoid being thought badly of by other people, and this is an admirable trait in any person.

# The Real Meaning Of Bunkai

The term *bunkai* has become very popular in recent years, and it pleases me greatly that more people are now interested in researching the meanings behind the techniques contained in *kata*. This was not always the case though, and when I first began training there was hardly any explanation provided for the various movements, and those which were given were almost completely useless. I should explain that I did not begin my training in Okinawan *Goju Ryu*, but in a Japanese *Kyokushinkai* derived school. This was not the fault of the *Kyokushin* approach though, because most schools at that time in the UK had little idea about how to effectively use *kata*.

A quick search on youtube will reveal just how popular the pursuit of finding applications for *kata* has now become, and in fact, many of today's '*karate* celebrities' owe their fame completely to their unique interpretations of *kata* movements. The more visually impressive these applications are, the more people will arrive at their door wanting to learn. As a result of this we see long strings of applications spliced together in order to create various drills which play out like an overly elaborate fight scene from a movie. Another recent innovation is the introduction of *bunkai* performances within team *kata* tournaments. These serve absolutely no purpose and should be done away with before this gets even more out of control than it already has. The applications demonstrated are always done so for visual effect and to impress an audience. Rarely do they pay any resemblance to the actual *kata* they are supposed to be from, hence the addition of *jodan yoko geri* in *suparinpei*, or jumping up on one opponent to then attack a second assailant. It is all quite ridiculous and any adult with half a brain would see that such games have nothing to do with *bujutsu*.

In my opinion the term *bunkai* suggests a lot more and carries with it an opportunity for greater growth as martial artists than we currently allow. The commonly used translation for the term *bunkai* is application, but a quick look in a *kanji* dictionary will reveal that the character used for *Bun* refers to 'a part, portion or share', whereas the *kanji* for *Kai* means 'to solve, understand, or explain'. When the two *kanji* are combined they mean 'decomposition, disassembly or analysis'. These terms conjure up a completely different mental image for me.

# 分解

The impression I get from the correct use of the term *bunkai* is one of an engineer taking apart a complicated machine in order to investigate how it works. The engineer will separate each component part and seek to understand everything about how it functions on its own. Following this he will research how each bit relates to the other parts of that same machine, how they fit together, and through trial and error he will discover what they can and cannot achieve. The process of reassembly will then begin and he will learn how the components interact and how each has an effect upon the overall usefulness of the machine. Through the lessons learnt during this process he will develop an in-depth understanding of his machine and be able to immediately know what is wrong, the causes, and how to fix it should it suddenly break down. In addition to this, he will also develop a greater understanding of how similar machines operate and be able to transfer his skills to other areas. Over time his skills will develop to the extent that he can guide others through this process and be able to troubleshoot other people's machines, offering solutions to their problems. Other people may be content to just use their machine until it breaks down, but when this happens an expert is needed.

This for me is the real meaning of *bunkai*.

The fighting application of a technique is only one very small part, and is in my opinion not even the most useful. Assigning set applications to a given movement is not only limiting, but it can also generate confusion and delay spontaneous response. If you say to a student 'this is the application for this movement', it will often stick in their head and they will find it difficult to use their own imagination to 'see' and 'feel' other possibilities for the same technique. Each movement has unlimited uses.

My friend Wade Chroninger *sensei* has a really nice saying '*kata* teaches implied technique'. This for me explains *kata* perfectly. *Kata* fine tunes the body so that it is able to react according to a given set of circumstances without conscious thought. Conscious thought is what causes the stutter between action and reaction and is what causes you to be hit, making it difficult to regain the initiative. Teaching set applications is very convenient for a beginner and can allow them to see the possibilities of how to apply *kata* against an opponent, but when it reaches the stage of 'if the opponent attacks with A, I will respond with B' this then becomes useless. Such pre-determined circumstances never appear in real life and learning *budo* in this way provides only a childlike comfort for the learner who develops faith that they will be able to use such techniques to overcome an adversary. If you try to apply *kata* in this way you are doomed to failure. In my opinion it is more beneficial to simply react and not think about it too much. The more you practice and the more you make the *kata* a part of you, the more the art will come alive through your responses. This is why *kakie* is such a useful training tool. In my approach I have students face each other in *kakie* and allow all strikes, holds and takedowns. Nothing is off limits, but of course there is control. Inevitably the students will be placed into various random situations which they must then figure a way out from. These instances are the moments where the usefulness of *kata* presents itself. Whether you have successfully escaped or not, it is important to then re-enact the movements without the training partner afterwards in order to discover how your instinctive movements related to the classical *kata*. This should then be analyzed in depth to discover what could have been done better. At first this may be difficult, but over time you will find that the 'feeling' of your response will correspond to a certain technique. When this happens it can be said that you have used *kata*. This is an approach I have used for many years and is something I do after every real life encounter. I do this as a way of 'de-briefing' myself and learning from my mistakes and successes. To date I have never consciously thought about using a particular technique, but the movement which my subconscious selects to respond with always comes from *kata*. In addition, every encounter I've had has always played out in accordance with '*mittsu no horitsu*', meaning that an encounter will be concluded within three techniques. This once again suggests against the requirement for long, complicated drills in my experience.

Having said all of this, the responses which the subconscious selects will amount to nothing if the body structure, power delivery method, use of *kamae* or body shifting, and effective set ups are not employed. This is where *bunkai* finds its real use.

The individual movements and postures of *kata* represent a mere snippet of the story. They can be likened to a still photograph taken from a 2 hour movie. It is impossible to tell the entire story from this one glimpse. The skill in learning how to use *kata* comes in being able to discern the 'before and after' of a given point. This can be likened to the engineer discovering how each of the individual parts fit together to make the whole machine operate. For example, *hiji ate* (elbow strike) appears frequently in the various *kata* of *Goju Ryu* in many different guises. Sometimes it punches forward, sometimes it scoops upward, sometimes it is delivered to the rear, and sometimes it is thrown along a horizontal plane. Another thing which has an effect is the stance from which the elbow is delivered, *zenkutsu dachi*, *neko ashi dachi* or *shiko dachi*. All these stances are used at some point, but each has an entirely different effect upon the overall use of the technique. Which techniques are used immediately prior to throwing the *hiji ate* in order to create the *suki* (opening)? Which technique is used immediately following the strike? What body movement is used to enter and withdraw from the opportunity to strike? Which target area is struck, how will this impact upon the opponent's structure and where they are likely to be immediately following our successful strike? Does the *kata* have an answer for what to do if our strike is defended, misses or does not have any effect on the opponent? These are just some of the considerations for a given movement and an example of what it means to disassemble or analyze. This is *bunkai*.

When we understand how to investigate a movement in accordance with the above in order to discover its essence, we learn what is important and what can be discarded. This allows for the individuality of a technique or *kata*, and provides the perfect setting for art to flourish. *Kata* does not come in a one size fits all manner. Every person is different both physically and mentally, and it precisely due to this that learning *karate* in the old days was always done on a one to one basis in accordance with the individual needs of a student. *Kata* would be selected for individual study due to a person's body type, life experience, personal circumstances, as well as their character, age and personality traits. *Kata* would also occasionally be modified around physical impairments, and in the case of experts, every repetition of a *kata* could be different depending upon what they were 'seeing' at the time of their performance. *Uraken uchi* is *uraken uchi*, but the circumstances of its delivery and the subsequent choice of target can vary greatly according to the person's imagination and experience.

An understanding of this is what separates the master from a novice; an engineer from somebody who is content to just use the machine that was given to them. The master engineer will ensure that *karate* is something which can be used by everyone who is willing to make an effort, not only those who are physically gifted enough to be able to assume any posture perfectly or move according to a given template without fault. This is elitist to the exclusion of others and is not what *karate* is about. *Karate* should, if studied correctly, enable weaker people to overcome a stronger adversary. It should enable a person of limited physical capabilities to push past their boundaries and use their bodies in a way they thought previously impossible. This is the real meaning of *bunkai* I think.

# Before And After The Battle

One of my pet hates is when I see a person lose their concentration at the end of a *kata*. No matter how well the *kata* may have been performed prior to returning to *yoi kamae*, if the *yoi* itself is rushed or lacking in intent, I will not be satisfied.

*Yoi* is not just a posture which one has to assume in the moments before and after a *kata*. Much more than this, *yoi* is a state of mind and an attitude. To perform only the physical movements without the accompanying emotional content is as useful as having a tea bag but no water. The *kanji* used to represent *yoi* give an interesting insight into its correct use. The kanji for **yo** means 'to use, take up, or adopt', whereas the character for *i* means 'intention, feeling, thought, or meaning'.

When used together the *kanji* translate as 'preparations or arrangements'. I find the singular use of the particular kanji more enlightening personally, and think they give a better clue into the actual application of *yoi*.

It is no exaggeration to say that the most important parts of the *kata* are the initial and final *yoi* positions. The importance of the beginning *yoi kamae* should be fairly obvious to most people. The moments leading up to an altercation are the most dangerous, and victory or defeat is often decided during this stage. If your mind is wandering elsewhere you will fail to notice that the opponent is setting you up for a pre-emptive strike, you may also miss whether he is armed or if his friend has sneaked around for a surprise attack from the side. How you position yourself in relation to the threats posed may help to improve your chances of affecting a successful escape, and your use of body language could lure the opponent into a false sense of superiority which could then be exploited. But, in order to achieve any of this, the correct mindset needs to be adopted. The most important aspect of this mental state is the ability to seize the initiative. This decisive frame of mind is what stops a person from becoming a victim and is something which can be used over an extremely long *ma'ai* in order to avoid coming into contact with a threat in the first place. Crossing the street and taking a different route home is an example of taking the initiative rather than waiting to be put into a difficult position from which you might have to fight your way out from. When something happens you must respond without hesitation and the earlier you do this, the more options you will have available to avoid conflict.

When adopting the position of *yoi* at the beginning of *kata* you should assume a positive mindset and be completely committed to controlling every moment which follows. During these moments it is appropriate to reassure yourself and think positively about what you wish to achieve. This part of *yoi* can be likened to an athlete psyching themselves up before a contest. The subtle physical and psychological changes which occur during this moment become stronger with experience, and with practice you will find yourself able to adopt the attitude of *yoi* instantly whenever faced with a threat or a challenging situation. When I find myself faced with a potentially dangerous incident in which I have time to think beforehand, I often use the hand position of *yoi* in order to steady my nerves and strengthen my resolve. This helps greatly to push negative thoughts aside and maintain focus upon the task at hand.

After the final technique of the *kata* has been completed, it is more important than ever to not allow your guard to drop. There is a saying 'after the battle is won, tighten your chinstrap'. The defeated opponent may draw a weapon, he may follow you home and attack you at a later stage, or maybe he has friends who have been watching from a distance? The possibilities are endless. It is also important to take stock of the situation and assess what else needs to be done. It is common during a physical confrontation that a person loses the ability to think rationally and a primal aggression takes over known as 'Red Mist'. This can result in striking an opponent more times than is necessary to defend yourself. For *karateka* such behavior poses moral problems, but in addition, it creates a difficult situation legally and may result in prosecution and imprisonment. Hurting another person or causing loss of life is something which will weigh heavily on your conscience for the rest of your life. The state of *yoi* provides an opportunity to seek clarity and assess the situation fully during the lull of the battle. Having the confidence to withdraw from the situation without causing unnecessary injury is a desirable trait in a *budoka*. When returning to *yoi kamae* at the end of *kata* you should still be exhibiting dominance over the opponent(s), however, caution must be maintained. Do not let your guard down until you are certain the battle is definitely over. When I see *yoi* being rushed I find it difficult to believe that the person has any appreciation of the mindset required for self-defence.

Having said this, do not value the appearance of *yoi* over the function. *Yoi* should not be pretty; it should be a frightening thing to witness. There is a difference between performing *yoi* slowly and performing *yoi* correctly.

It all comes down to the attitude of the individual. The more experience you gain in your studies, the more depth you can then add to the postures in order to display the correct mental attributes.

I find it quite interesting that Miyagi Chojun *sensei* changed the beginning *yoi kamae* from the original *heiko dachi* position with the fists held at the side of the body during the later years of his life. By making the start and finish of *kata* identical I believe that Miyagi *sensei* has sent a clever warning to all students of his art. At both the beginning and the ending of a situation there should be no difference in your attitude; both are equally dangerous periods. Do not allow yourself to become sloppy and lose concentration, even for a moment.

**Practicing in extreme weather conditions can enhance your appreciation of Yoi**

# Kata According To The Elements

For as long as I can remember in my studies of *Goju Ryu*, I have always been interested in how Miyagi Chojun *sensei* conducted his *kata* training in accordance with the flow of nature. This would affect not only how he practiced during the changing of the seasons, but also where he trained, the compass direction he faced, and even which *kata* he concentrated upon depending upon the time of day. Higaonna Morio *sensei* wrote regarding this;

*'Miyagi was continually adjusting his training and surroundings in order to correspond with the changing seasons, training sometimes in the mountains, at other times on the beach and so forth.'* [7]

Higaonna *sensei* went on further to say;

*'He researched each kata in great depth, practicing not only the techniques, but also each kata at a specific time during the day.'*

This was one of the first books I read regarding *Goju Ryu*, and these brief mentions of Miyagi *sensei's* training habits have retained my curiosity ever since. Figuring out how Miyagi *sensei* did this has been a puzzle which has kept me researching for many years, never quite finding the answer. On one occasion I asked Higaonna Morio *sensei* directly about this and he told me that in order to get the most from each *kata* they should be practiced at a certain time of day. He advised that *Sanchin* and *Tensho* should always be practiced with the sun to your rear and that a person's energy levels are at their lowest around 4am and 4pm. Unfortunately I was unable to pursue this line of questioning any further at that time. A few years later I asked Hokama Tetsuhiro *sensei* whether *Sanchin* is best practiced at a certain time of day in order to check if my research was on the right track, but he replied that it did not matter. However, a few days following this incident he began to speak in depth about the *Ekkinkyo* and *Suizenkyo* texts in relation to my original question. On another occasion we were in the Fukushuen in Kume together, crossing a bridge which has stone carvings of the different animals of the Chinese zodiac. I took this opportunity to ask him about the *embusen* of *kata* and how *Suparinpei* pays particular attention to the 8 compass points. His response to this was particularly interesting because he spoke in terms of the 5 Element theory and how the left leg in *Suparinpei* acts as 'earth'. This pushed my research in a slightly different direction and gave me the hint I needed to start finding some answers for my questions.

---

[7] The History of Karate, Higaonna Morio, p57

So far I have been unable to find anybody who has been able to solve the puzzle of which kata suits which time of day definitively. As frustrating as this may be, it has also been a blessing. Through my pursuit of information on this matter I have been forced to research many different texts from various martial arts which I probably would have never seen under other circumstances. My research has led me from the Okinawan arts, to those of Japan, China, India, Malaysia, Thailand and even as far as Greece and Egypt. I've had an opportunity to learn about medicine, geomancy, folk beliefs and religions, astrology and ancient history. Although in some ways I feel I will never solve this puzzle 100%, at least my journey has enabled me to broaden my horizons and learn about some of the things which affected the daily activities of those living during the time of *Karate's* initial development. This in itself is a far greater gift than what I had originally set out for.

Some basic research into the way the Chinese viewed nature will quickly reveal the concepts of *Yin Yang* and the 5 Elements. The importance of these two theories cannot be overlooked for they shaped literally every aspect of life in ancient China and its surrounding nations. It is said that creation came from the separation of the *Wuji* (whole) into *Yin Yang* (duality). Duality further divided into the 5 Elements, and from this, all things evolved. *Yin Yang* and the 5 Elements are ancient Taoist theories which provide a template for diagnosing and treating illness both in the body and in a person's surroundings. The latter use of these theories is referred to as *Feng Shui*. The act of balancing these energies in one's body and local environment promotes health and good fortune. Even today in the expat Chinese communities of Taiwan, Indonesia, and Malaysia, it is common that expert martial artists will also be doctors or *Feng Shui* consultants, and the local people will visit them with various ailments or to seek advice about their personal circumstances.

Despite the ancient practices of Taoism being almost eradicated during the Chinese Cultural Revolution, the relationship between the Chinese internal arts and Taoism remains a close one. It is my opinion that the origins of *kata* as a linked sequence of movements organized around a geometric template can be found in ancient Taoist purification rituals such as the 'Dance On The Stars'. Kristofer Schipper writes concerning this tradition;

*'he traces with his limping walk the outline of the Dipper constellation in the middle of the ritual area.'*[8]

---

[8] The Taoist Body, Kristofer Schipper, p98

The Dance On The Stars is believed by some to have evolved from the ancient Shamanistic ritual known as 'The Steps Of Yu'.

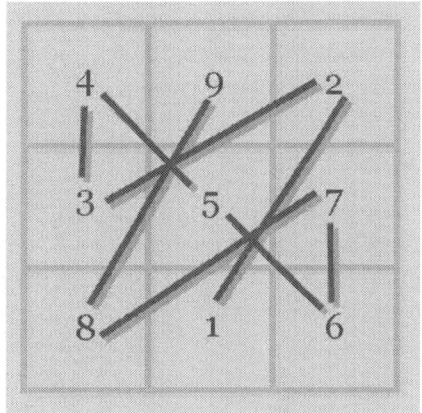

*The basic Steps of Yu involved three steps and nine traces. Later they diversified into different types, called Twelve Traces and Three-Five Traces.*
*The three steps and nine traces of the Steps of Yu were thought to have the shape of the Big Dipper, so they were associated with Pacing the Big Dipper.'* [9]

It can be seen described above how a set sequence of movements was arranged around a defined number of steps in specific directions. These movements were also accompanied by various hand positions which were believed to evoke certain celestial energies. Such rituals were performed to summon the gods and deities and were conducted during religious festivals as well as on auspicious occasions such as births, weddings and funerals in order to bring good fortune to those concerned. I feel quite certain that these ancient rituals formed the basis of *kata* as we know it today. Although it is said that *Sanchin* can be practiced with as many steps as space allows, a set order has been handed down which limits the number of steps to three forward and three back for formal practice. Most other *kata* also contain a high frequency of 3 repetitions for a given technique. Some *kata* face 4 compass directions, whereas other turn through 8. There are also various postures within the *kata* which correspond to exactly to Buddhist hand positions such as *mawashi uke* where the top hand represents fearlessness and the bottom hand compassion. The famous Taoist deity *Busaganashi* which was revered by Miyagi Chojun *sensei* displays the Taoist 'sword fingers' hand formation which is used to eradicate evil from the body. It can be difficult to truly appreciate how life was viewed during the pre-technological age from which the martial arts evolved, but such superstitions were so intertwined with the daily lives of the people concerned that it is inevitable that these beliefs would eventually find their way into the formal practices and routines of the martial arts. For example, Miyagi Chojun *sensei* would devote every 1st and 15th lunar day to the worship of *Busaganashi*. The 1st and 15th lunar date is very important in Taoist folklore as well as in the practice of *Qigong* according to the *Ekkinkyo* and *Suizenkyo* texts which state these to be the times when it is possible to balance the energies of

---

[9] Michael Winn, http://forum.healingdao.com/philosophy/message/11415%5C

*Yin* and *Yang* most effectively. Miyagi *sensei* was also known to have been particularly influenced by the *Bubishi*, and in particular the *Kenpo Hakku* from which he drew the name for his art. One of the lines in the *Kenpo Hakku* reads;

*'our blood circulation parallels the solar and lunar cycles of each day'*[10]

I first believed that this referred to the attacking of vital points as outlined elsewhere in the *Bubishi*, and this may well still be the case; however, if we consider the sun to be *Yang* and the moon *Yin*, it can be argued that the phrase relates to the flow of energy around the body as influenced by the time of day. I believe this is what Higaonna *sensei* was referring to when he mentioned about a person's energy levels peaking and falling at certain times. Both of these theories are one and the same, but one concerns using the concept to cause harm, whereas the other is used in order to promote good health within our bodies.

The 24 hour period of a day corresponds with *Yin* and *Yang* as follows;

12am – *Yin*

6am - *Yin* becoming *Yang*

12pm – *Yang*

6pm – *Yang* becoming *Yin*

It has been said that *Sanchin* is best practiced at 6am, 12pm and 6pm in order to balance *Yin* and *Yang*. *Yin* is produced naturally in the body whereas *Yang* depletes with age and needs to be maintained through training. In addition to this, by strengthening our *Yang* energy, *Yin* is also enhanced. This can be likened to the action of a pendulum; the higher it rises on one side, the higher it will swing on the opposite side.

The changing states of *Yin* and *Yang* can be further divided according to the 5 Elements and compass directions.

12am – *Yin*/Water/North

6am – *Yin-Yang*/Wood/East

12pm – *Yang*/Fire/South

6pm – *Yang-Yin*/Metal/West

Earth is located at the points where *Yin* changes to *Yang* and *Yang* to *Yin*. Earth can be considered the stabilizing

---

[10] Bubishi, Patrick McCarthy, p159

element.

Further to this, the changing of the seasons also follows this pattern as follows;

Winter – *Yin*/Water/North

Spring – *Yin-Yang*/Wood/East

Summer – *Yang*/Fire/South

Autumn – *Yang-Yin*/Metal/West

In relation to this theory, it is my current opinion that the *kata* of *Goju Ryu* can be assigned an element which best represents their overall character. The seed for this idea was planted by Hokama *sensei* when he mentioned about the left foot corresponding with Earth in *Suparinpei*. I was also very excited when I read the book 'College of Chinese Martial Arts Training Manual' by Paul Brecher. This book contained a number of references to how the forms found in *Bagua* and *Hsing-I* correspond with one of the 5 Elements and a specific time of day or direction. It has been frequently mentioned in *Goju Ryu* circles that Miyagi *sensei* developed a keen interest into the Chinese internal styles during his travels, and I wonder whether it was due to his interaction with the practitioners of these arts that his thinking and training methods were influenced in this way.

Working on this theory, I began to investigate by 'feel' which *kata* best corresponded to each of the 5 Elements. My findings are as follows;

### *Saifa* – Metal

The evasive body movements of this *kata* remind me of the piercing thrusts and flowing slashes of a sword. Displaying an outer firmness which belies its inner flexibility, *Saifa* best represents *Yang* changing to *Yin*, and relies more on evasiveness and subtlety than brute strength and dominance. The footwork suggests a light *Ju* floating method of stepping on occasions, and a powerful *Go* anchoring on others. The applications of *Saifa* encourage disengaging from an opponent and repelling their advances by attacking their vulnerable points with piercing hand positions which penetrate the target such as *haito uchi* and *hira ken*. As the name 'smash and tear' suggests, there are multiple points where you rip, pull, tear and shred at the opponent, much like the slashes of the deadly *kama*.

### *Seiunchin* – Earth

Displaying a bold confidence, *Seiunchin* embodies the character of Earth, representing grounding, dominance, uprooting and unbalancing, generated by the low postures and sure footwork throughout. The initial posture of the *kata* known as *'yama kamae'* displays the calm, immovable nature of a mountain. The applications of *Seiunchin kata* encourage

 drawing an opponent in close, breaking their posture and then destroying with close range strikes. Making frequent use of *shiko dachi* and with an absence of overt kicking techniques, *Seiunchin* provides a strong connection with the ground and best displays the characteristics of Earth.

### *Shisochin* – Wood

*Shisochin* is a very balanced *kata* which concentrates its movements along the 4 directions. Making frequent use of *zenkutsu dachi* throughout to reach into and penetrate an opponent's defenses, the various postures of *Shisochin* mimic the branches of a tree reaching toward the sun, with its roots of penetrating the earth below. Displaying flexibility in its movements throughout, the *kata* blends hard and soft wonderfully, yet still maintains a firm grounding. The assertive movements of the *kata* grow outward from small to large, expanding from short stances to longer postures, best characterizing *Yin* changing to *Yang*.

### *Sanseiru* – Fire

*Sanseiru* is relentless in its dominance of the opponent. Chasing throughout and putting the opponent on the back foot, *Sanseiru* does not allow the opponent an opportunity to settle and regain the initiative. Assertive and aggressive in its nature, *Sanseiru* characterizes a fire engulfing anything which stands in its way. At the conclusion of the *kata*, everything slows and settles into a grounded posture, the flames die down and the ashes fall providing a balance of action and inaction.

### *Seipai* – Water

This *kata* is grounded and settled whilst maintaining a balanced flow throughout. At various points in the *kata*, the body twists and spirals in order to generate great centrifugal force, like the motions of a whirlpool. Loose *Ju* type strikes are prevalent which release the force through the target to shock the internal organs. The postures of the *kata* rise and fall like the crashing of a wave, and on occasions the distance is closed quickly with light footwork concluding in firmness, with strong upper body power to crash into the opponent using body checks. These movements resemble the strong surging of water, powering through anything in its path.

## *Kururunfa* – Water

*Kururunfa* is the sister of *Seipai*. Containing many of the same principles of body movement and power generation, this *kata* has a lighter feel to it than its heavier brother. As such, these two *kata* can be considered the *Yin* and *Yang* of the *Ju* water element. An alternate translation of the *kanji* for this *kata* is 'come stay the waves, peacefulness and tearing'. Like an ocean, the *kata* contains elements of calmness, combined with frightening displays of power. The *age tsuki, mae geri & hiji ate* combination surges forward like a tsunami before quietly and calmly withdrawing into *tenchi kamae*. The body position frequently changes between high and low postures, mimicking the gentle flow of water.

## *Seisan* – Fire

This *kata* is upright, mobile, fast and assertive throughout. It makes frequent use of combination attacks to overwhelm the opponent's defenses and maintain the initiative. *Seisan* is the most pressing of the *Goju Ryu kata*, using *suri ashi* to close long distances and dart boldly in to thwart an attack at its origin, whilst multiple strikes engulf and tie up the opponent. The striking techniques used throughout are forceful *Go* type attacks designed to crush and smash the target area. *Seisan* can be considered the sister to *Sanseiru*. Both are fire elements, but *Sanseiru* is the more grounded and forceful of the two, whereas *Seisan* adopts a more upright, mobile posture and utilizes speed and multiple strikes over power, making it the *Ju* partner to *Sanseiru's Go* in the Fire element.

## *Suparinpei* – Earth

This *kata* is well balanced in both technique and tempo. The movements advance and return around a single point, whilst turning through multiple directions in a counter clockwise rotation to face all 8 gates. Its striking methods are forceful and deliberate, delivered with a confidence and determination to make every strike capable of finishing the opponent with a single blow. Both high and low postures are used throughout, and the performer steadily holds his ground. *Suparinpei* is twinned with *Seiunchin* in the Earth element brother/sister relationship and provides the *Go* to *Seiunchin's Ju*.

The elements, feelings and imagery attached to each *kata* here are only my opinions based on my own personal experiences with the *kata*. Regarding the 5 Elements it is common even for experts to disagree about the properties attached to each element, and this leads me to believe that such training was a personal approach of Miyagi *sensei* rather than something which was mainstream and known by everyone at that time. It is also highly probable that he did not share these theories with anybody else for his whole approach to *karate* and teaching appears to have been geared toward students finding their own answers rather than him giving everything away.

So, having found for myself a workable theory for this, what does it all mean? The lifestyles of 99% of people would mean that training according to such a structure would be near impossible, so it would be difficult to discover if such an approach to training would have any real benefit. In my opinion, the main use of this can be found in the assigning of *tokui kata* (specialty kata). In the past, students were assigned a *kata* for their own personal study. This *kata* would be chosen according to their body type, strengths and weaknesses, character and personality traits, and according to some sources, even birth date and genealogy were considered. Interestingly, according to the 5 Element theory, every person can be categorized according to an Element which describes their body type, personality and character. For example Wood body types are generally tall and thin with a strength that belies their appearance. Fire body types are short, fast and energetic and can be easily angered. Earth body types are easy going and have powerful legs and a heavy build. If we consider this theory in relation to the Elements assigned to the *kata* above we can begin to see how a specific *kata* might better suit an individual, and how the tactical methods of that *kata* might be specifically geared toward utilizing the natural strengths of that person.

In addition to this, we could also consider how a particular *kata* might assist in developing areas which are naturally weaker in a person. For example, a person who is overly passive and easy to take advantage of might have Water in excess. In order to address this balance, a Fire *kata* such as *Sanseiru* or *Seisan* might have been assigned in order to strengthen the Fire element and address the natural balance. On a less esoteric level this is simply a case of teaching a naturally shy person to be more outgoing and confident through developing the natural traits instilled by that *kata*.

With regards to physical and emotional health, it is also possible that the *kata* could be used as a way of self-healing and attaining balance from imbalance. Wherever there is an excess or deficiency in one of the elements, this often results in illness. Each of the elements relates to an internal organ and certain character traits. Traditional Chinese medicine works on this theory. A person who has a deficiency in Wood for example may display symptoms of restlessness, lack of creative interest, severe depression, muscle weakness, etc. A person deficient in Wood struggles to make decisions or take control of a situation, never getting their ideas off the ground. In Chinese medicine, a common way of treating Wood deficiency is to strengthen the elements of Wood and Water. In the 5 Element theory, Water is the mother of Wood and so can be used to increase the strength of its child element. Could the *kata* be used in this way to treat illness and emotional disorder? This would require research from experts in Traditional Chinese Medicine, but for me it provides an exciting avenue for future research.

Concerning this subject, it has been said from many different sources that Miyagi *sensei* favored *Shisochin kata* in his personal practice toward the final years of his life, stating that this *kata* best suited his body during that time. The symptoms described above in relation to Wood deficiency also illustrate Miyagi *sensei*'s physical and emotional condition during the later stages of his life following WW2. That he chose to focus upon *Shisochin* could be merely coincidental, but I find it very interesting nonetheless.

The thoughts presented in this article are only my personal findings in relation to this subject, and my research is still at a very early stage and subject to change as I learn more. I sincerely hope though, that this slightly different approach to looking at *kata* will inspire further interest and research from experts who might be able to raise our general understanding and shed further light upon the relationship between *kata* and nature.

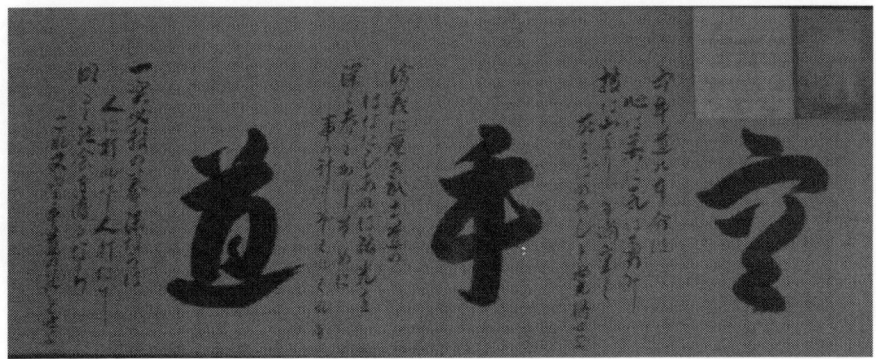

# **Eggs**

I enjoy scrambled eggs for breakfast sometimes, especially if I'm not the one making them. You see, whenever I eat out for breakfast at a café or restaurant, the scrambled eggs are always excellent, but when I try to make them, they are usually very dry and tasteless. I have been trying to improve my scrambled eggs for many years now, but still they are not very good. A few days ago my friend who keeps chickens gave me some fresh eggs from some of his hens which he had collected that morning. I took them home and made scrambled eggs out of them the following day and guess what, they were just as good as the ones in the café.

It appears that the problem had been caused by me using eggs which were simply not up to the task. If the ingredients are not very good to begin with, the outcome will probably be disappointing. The trouble is, from the outside appearance, an egg looks pretty much the same as any other egg. Sometimes we can get a better idea about where the eggs came from by the packaging, but if this information is not particularly accurate, or is exaggerated in order to make them more appealing, we still run the risk of getting poor eggs despite our best efforts.

With the fresh eggs my friend gave me, I was initially taken aback by how different they looked once I had broken through the outer shell. Inside the yolk was much brighter, so much so that I thought something might be wrong with them! The good quality eggs looked strange compared to the average ones I was used to, but the end result was incomparable.

Whilst I was stuffing my face with my breakfast I got thinking about *karate* and how similar my egg situation had been to the dilemma faced by many sincere practitioners around the world. For the beginner, no matter how well researched they are on the subject of *karate*; from the outer appearance, *karate* is just *karate*. It can be difficult for the novice to tell the genuine *dojo* from the poor imitations, especially when the websites and advertisements claim respectable credentials and authentic lineages, as they always seem to do. The sad thing is, no matter how hard the student tries, if the original ingredients of the *dojo* are not of a good quality, the end result will suffer. This can eventually lead to disillusionment and the student losing interest and abandoning their study.

Finding a good *dojo* requires a great deal of effort and research from the student, but also, I regret to say, a little luck. Acceptance into a genuine *dojo* is not a foregone conclusion, and even if one is allowed to train, when faced with the harsh reality of studying under such circumstances, many students might discover that actually, *karate* is not for them.

The vast majority of *karate* on offer these days is of the 3K variety. This approach to training has its benefits, especially when teaching large groups a set syllabus which everybody is expected to follow in order to advance through the ranks. This is only one type of *karate* though, and is the kind which is taught to high school students who do not have the maturity, attention span or motivation to take control of their own development. For beginners this method of training is ok, but is a 40 year old father the same as a 14 year old schoolboy? Where is the room for personal growth and individuality? Once the syllabus is completed and the student has achieved their desired rank, where else is there to go with their training? In my opinion this is why so many *karate* practitioners are seeking more than what their current *dojo* offers, hence the popularity of the various seminars, books and DVD's from *karate's* 'celebrity' teachers. Even amongst the people who have moved away from 3K *karate*, many are poor clones of whichever celebrity they choose to emulate. They are still trying to replicate the dishes of master chefs with poor base ingredients, and attempting to cook them in kitchens which are not fit for purpose.

If the student is lucky enough to find an authentic *karate dojo*, the student is then faced with a number of questions to answer. Do they stay within their comfort zone where it is possible to hide in the line-up surrounded by other students? Do they pay their *dojo* fees each week, train for a couple of hours and feel content that they have fulfilled their obligation as a student? Do they follow a structured syllabus, safe in the knowledge that their progression has already been taken care of by somebody else who will decide what they learn, and when, despite having probably never met them or been aware of their personal circumstances and ability to learn? Can they submit themselves to continual scrutiny, observation, correction and the pressure of knowing that *karate* is not something they can just pick up and put down whenever they attend or leave the *dojo*? Can they take control of their training and their lives, allowing nobody to make excuses for them, nor offering any of themselves? Can they motivate themselves to get on and train although nobody is watching and nobody will truthfully know whether they have trained or stayed indoors in the warm instead? Depending on how the student answers these questions, the eventual outcome of their training will be very different, and the experiences felt along the way will shape their character and give their *karate* purpose and a greater depth. Through this they will learn the true value of *karatedo*.

They say 'eggs is eggs', but I disagree. If the base ingredients are not up to the task, how can we ever hope to create a dish which tastes as good as we might expect? Then again, if all you have ever eaten is rotten eggs for breakfast, perhaps you might acquire a taste for them in the end?

# Jishin

One of the greatest gifts that *karatedo* can bestow upon the practitioner is *Jishin* (self-confidence). This one thing can have a huge positive influence over all areas of life. As a child I was quite outgoing, but not particularly confident by any means. The demons of self-doubt haunted me throughout my teenage years and I frequently felt the need to get myself noticed in order to boost my ego. I wanted other people to tell me I was good at something because I never really believed in myself. *Karate* was the only thing I ever really felt a connection with, something I had a certain degree of natural ability for. Please understand I am not saying this to show off, it is just that I was completely hopeless at most other physical activities and upon beginning *karate,* it was such a relief to find something that I could actually do to a half acceptable standard.

It is difficult to know what kind of person I would have become if not for *karate*, because I have been practicing for most of my life so will never know any different. I sometimes wonder though if I would have been capable of achieving some of the things I have, had I not developed self-confidence through training.

When I was a teenager confrontation absolutely terrified me, to the point of whenever I was faced with aggression I would freeze and be unable to offer any sort of response or escape. I would just hide within myself and hope it all went away. Immediately afterwards I would be beating myself up mentally for being unable to do anything and for being too afraid. This applied not only to fighting, but also to other areas of difficulty such as job interviews, public speaking, meeting new people or even getting girlfriends. I realize I must be painting a picture here that I was a real loser during my youth!!! In short, I had an image in my mind of what I thought I could achieve, but my character lacked the strength to make these images a reality. My father was a very strong natural fighter, as were his brothers and my grandfather. As a youth I felt I needed to live up to this and become strong to make them proud. In hindsight I realize how silly this was, but youthful heads are always full of strange ideas.

The *karate* I had been training in up until this point was the same kind practiced by the vast majority of *karateka* around the world. I would attend a hired hall twice a week where I would be put through my paces, performing various techniques up and down the *dojo* to the count of the instructor. There would also be *kata* with no application and standard light contact *kumite* to finish. This was very comfortable training and I soon reached the point where there was nowhere else for me to go within this particular kind of *karate*. I hear this same dilemma from many practitioners all over the world who are all looking for more to *karate* than that offered in the standard 3k variety. I decided that I would go to Okinawa to look for true *karate*, but in order to do this I would first need to learn 'authentic' Okinawan *karate* rather than what I was currently studying. This idea led me to request to become a student of Richard Barrett *sensei*.

After my first lesson from Barrett *sensei* I immediately knew I had made a mistake. The training at his *dojo* was much harder than that I had been used to, and I almost passed out and vomited due to the 'warm up'. I wished that I had chosen another *dojo* instead! My first year as his student had such an impact upon me that I honestly think it shaped my current circumstances in life.

Barrett sensei's *dojo* was one hour's drive from my parents' house where I was living at the time. During the journey I would be thinking of all sorts of excuses to turn around and miss training. Perhaps I could say my car had broken down, or I was ill. All of these things would be coming into my head as the butterflies in the pit of my stomach became stronger the  closer I got. Once at his house it was too late, and as soon as I stepped foot into the *dojo* the hardest part was over. I was stuck there with no chance of escape so that particular battle was finished, but a number of different battles would then begin as I once more came to face my true nature through training. In retrospect, the training probably wasn't as hard as I remember; our achievements sometimes get exaggerated in our minds over time I think. The things I felt during training though are only too real. Although I only see my teacher a few times a year now, the same feelings sometimes come back during the flights out to Spain when I visit him. These feelings are more welcome these days though for they contain many good memories.

Did this training make my *karate* any better? Maybe, maybe not? A more relaxed learning atmosphere may be more conducive to producing better results with regard to technical ability, perhaps. Training in Okinawa was also quite a relaxed affair in comparison. Such intense training would probably also be frowned upon from a sports science perspective as on many occasions correct form and technique would deteriorate completely as I struggled my way through whatever the particular exercise was. What cannot be doubted for a moment though is that I came out of that first year a completely different person to the one who first walked into that *dojo*. I was no longer afraid. This does not mean I became tough, it just meant that I developed the ability to just get on with it and not listen to the negative voices which tried to hold me back from whatever I wanted to achieve. When you continue to do 'just one more, just one more', the positive voices learn to shout louder than the negative ones. You learn to counter 'I can't' with 'I can'. This is the most important lesson I've ever learnt from my *sensei*.

*Jishin* is revealed in the way we carry ourselves. Criminals work with a predatory mindset, selecting victims who they believe to be weaker than them and thus able to offer less resistance and give them less chance of failure and subsequent arrest. A person with natural *Jishin* is rarely singled out unless the criminal is particularly desperate. A person who is withdrawn into themselves lacks awareness, making them vulnerable for approach. Upon contact, if the intended victim continues to shrink away and display signs of defeat the criminal will press home their attack. This same phenomena is seen everywhere in the animal world. When two dogs prepare to fight, the victor is obvious from the outset from the posture of the animals. One will dominate; the other will cower and withdraw. This is nature. I do not know of any predators other than man who hunt tiger or shark? *Jishin* promotes *Yoi*, which in turn promotes *Kamae*, *Zanshin* and *Ma'ai*. These are the most important components of self-defense. Without first developing *Jishin*, the other areas will be ineffective.

When students enter the *dojo* they are required to perform *rei* whilst saying *'onegaishimasu'*. This is of course very important to show respect and courtesy, but also, this single action develops the student's appreciation of *Jishin*. If the student bows without confidence it can be seen in their eyes and posture. If the *'onegaishimasu'* lacks conviction and assertiveness, this is also easy to hear. By drawing the student's attention to these areas they begin to learn about how to carry themselves correctly in order to display confidence. This should not be confused with arrogance, as this can also single a person out as a victim or somebody not to be trusted. A confident posture and voice is a great asset to the student, not only from a self-defense point of view, but also when it comes to job interviews, work presentations, leadership and public speaking. Many people are afraid of confronting these things, but a *karateka* should be able to excel under such circumstances because of their training. This can lead to successful careers and personal relationships.

# Hitting The Target

One of the biggest complaints about traditional martial arts and their associated practice methods is that they lack realism and bear little resemblance to real fighting. Such criticism often comes from proponents of MMA or RBSD schools, but also a lot more frequently from people who do not practice any form of martial art at all or perhaps had limited experience of them during their youth. We really do ourselves no favors though, because the vast majority of what is taught as traditional martial arts these days is complete rubbish. When I see the various videos that are posted on youtube of 'street effective' techniques, or see the 'team *bunkai* performances' which have become popular at *kata* tournaments, I can't help but despair at what goes on in some people's heads.

Having said this, I am also too often left equally bewildered when I see the methods of some RBSD schools and their take on dealing with violence. In many cases it is painfully obvious that the person demonstrating has no clue about the nature of fighting, the mentality required for it, or the brains to avoid it in the first place. In the vast majority of cases it is all about showing off how tough they are rather than the actual content of the techniques.

Classical Okinawan *Karate* works just fine for civilian self-defense and law enforcement officers, but the training methods have to reflect the circumstances you will find yourself in. *Kumite* bears absolutely zero reflection to real fighting and is a waste of time. Many *karateka* build a false sense of confidence in their abilities due to their proficiency in *kumite*. Sure, maybe they can bang it out in the *dojo* with heavy contact, but the range and the circumstances are completely different from when you are taken by surprise by an attack from the rear on a dark night and the opponent is right on top of you giving you little space to move or react. *Bunkai* training too, although interesting, is largely irrelevant to real fighting. Practicing with a partner will have you reacting to unrealistic attacks and pulling your responses short to avoid hurting your training partner. I know there are many people out there with training methods which are said to reflect the circumstances of real fighting, but I honestly do not think it is possible to replicate it completely and I'm not convinced of the value of creating a habit of intentionally missing with strikes. Neither is it possible to practice these methods full power against your partner as this will obviously lead to injuries. It is a difficult dilemma isn't it?

There are people out there in the world who are naturally good at fighting. This has nothing to do with their level of skill, and to a certain extent it doesn't have much to do with their tactics, although some can use deception incredibly well to create an opening. The biggest thing which separates such people from the rest of us is that they have absolutely no regard for their opponent. They will think nothing of smashing a glass into your throat, gouging out an eye, stamping on your face whilst you are on the floor, or stabbing a knife into you multiple times until you are no longer moving. They will do this without an ounce of remorse, and often without giving it a second thought. Some of them will do this with little provocation and no warning. There is no such thing as a fair fight and the romantic image that fighting holds in the minds of many martial artists is a complete fantasy. Never are you the heroic victor standing proudly above your defeated opponent. The realities of victory and defeat are much more vulgar.

A fight is something you can taste. It has its own smell. It will leave you feeling dirty and have you questioning every single thing you did once it is all over. That is unless you are a thug without a conscience. I have never once been proud of myself for defeating an opponent and it is sometimes very difficult to return to the *dojo* the following day to continue training. I am often in conflict with my conscience and the lessons which I have learnt from fighting have come at a very heavy price on occasions. I say this not to sound tough, but because I believe it is very important that followers of the martial arts actually understand the realities of fighting and the consequences which come with it. If you understand the consequences properly, it becomes less likely that you will engage in fighting and will take every step possible to avoid conflict. This is the spirit of *karate*.

Some of the techniques contained within *kata* have the potential to finish the opponent immediately, leaving them with severe injuries. There are techniques which will break an opponent's neck, locks which can dislocate joints, strikes which can smash bones, and finger strikes which can cause permanent blindness. These techniques, although extremely severe, have the potential to save your life should you ever have the misfortune to be confronted by an opponent who is intent on ending your life and preventing you from returning home to your family. But ask yourself this; although you practice these techniques in *kata*, could you actually deliver them with full intent on a live opponent? Please do not be in a rush to answer this question. Take a little time to give it some serious thought.

S.L.A Marshall conducted a study into soldiers during WW2 and found that only 15% of infantrymen were actually trying to kill the enemy. These claims are widely disputed, but it raises some interesting issues nonetheless. This does not mean that 85% of the soldiers stood around doing nothing, it just identified that out of a group of people trained in the same methods only a small fraction had the ability and mentality to actively engage their opponent with the intent of killing them. From the remaining 85% there would have been a small number of men who would have frozen through fear, incapable of firing their weapon. There would have been a higher figure who tried to look busy, firing blind in the general direction of the enemy. There would also have been those who took aim at the enemy, only to then purposely aim off target to avoid killing them. Only the 15% took a deliberate aimed shot at their enemy. This for me has interesting implications for martial artists and deserves serious consideration.

In self-defense some people will freeze and allow the opponent to completely dominate them. Some people will react in a wild, panicked manner, lashing out with no thought to the techniques used or the targets struck. A small minority will enjoy the opportunity to test their skills and will take delight in defeating their opponent. In addition to this, I think there will be a percentage of martial artists who might find themselves in a vulnerable position but with a clear opportunity to use a technique which instantly finishes their opponent and makes escape possible, but despite this, they choose not to take the opportunity and consciously deliver a less effective strike instead. I have no statistics or intelligent sounding quotes to back up this theory, it is just my own thoughts based upon how I have reacted in past experiences, and from what I have observed in other people around me. However, since my training has become largely solitary over recent years with a heavy emphasis upon conditioning I have noticed some interesting and occasionally concerning results.

When I engage an opponent I do not view them as a human being, they are just a target. In my training I strike the *machiwara*, the wooden *tou*, rocks and the punch bag. These are just targets and I face them with the intent of defeating my opponent with a single blow. I have found that in real life, where an opening presents itself I will hit it without conscious thought with whatever technique fits the circumstances. I think that hitting the various striking implements on a regular basis somehow desensitizes the mind and removes the association between the strikes and their effect upon the human body. When training with a partner you associate the act of throwing a strike with pulling a strike short in order to avoid damaging your friend. You make an association between the target and a human being. By training with the conditioning tools you associate throwing the technique with the intent of hitting through the target. This becomes naturally 'how' you strike and removes the mental act of having to decide to hit the target. The body and mind become conditioned to always hitting the target. There is no recognition of the fact that the target is a person, it's just another target. There is of course a valid requirement for training with a partner, but I don't think it plays as big a part in preparing for self-defense as many people believe.

Along with *kata* practice and an appreciation of the mental attributes required for self-defense, I believe that the regular practice of hitting various striking tools is essential not only to correctly condition the parts of the body which will receive impact upon connecting with a target, but also in developing and conditioning the bodies responses to occur without conscious thought upon seeing an opportunity. When the responses become live and occur naturally it brings a much greater appreciation of why so much emphasis is placed upon developing good character traits and avoiding conflict to the best of your abilities.

**Richard Barrett** *sensei* **and Mike Clarke** *sensei* facing the *Machiwara*

# Accepting Criticism

Performing *kata* is a very strange thing. When I am alone I often find that I perform *kata* completely differently to when I am in front of a senior. When practicing during my home training I am never nervous, never unsure of the movements, and generally feel quite comfortable with the *kata* as though it is an old familiar friend; however, when I am asked by my *sensei* to perform a *kata* for him to critique, everything becomes rushed, cumbersome and tense; the exact opposite of what I want my *karate* to be these days. I do not get too disheartened by this though, for I know that I am not alone in this problem. I see the same thing happen to my own students when they perform *kata* for me, and many of my friends have mentioned that similar things happen to them under the same circumstances. All one can do is try their best.

There are a number of lessons to be learnt from these experiences such as coping under moderate levels of stress, dealing with anxiety, blocking out non-essential thoughts and 'fully committing to the moment', but even though we might be aware of the benefits of facing these emotions, there are still the moments following the *kata* where you say to yourself 'I should have done better'. This is a good thing I think, and serves to keep our feet on the ground and head out of the clouds. The day we believe we have mastered *karate* is the day we should give up altogether.

Prior to my first visit to Okinawa I was advised by my *sensei* to work hard, be polite, and accept criticism gratefully. To be corrected and criticized for your performance of *kata* is a good thing and you should greedily steal as much advice as you can from your seniors. I have very fond memories of training at the *Jundokan dojo* and having my *kata* picked apart by many wonderful teachers. Rather than feeling hopeless I saw this as an opportunity to learn and filled up many notebooks with great advice on the technical details of *kata*. Minor variations between practitioners of the same *dojo* led to interesting questions about the reasons, and these questions still hold my interest many years later. Often a piece of advice offered at the time but not really understood suddenly makes sense in a slightly different context or with older eyes. My point is, do not become despondent if your technique is corrected. To be offered critique means that a senior thinks highly enough of you to want to spend their own time helping you develop into a better *karateka*.

On the flip side, if you are offered no critique then you can either take this to mean that your *kata* is perfect, or you might actually want to start wondering 'what have I done wrong?' In traditional *dojo*, if a student is not very well thought of they will simply be ignored. In more extreme cases they will be asked to leave the *dojo* altogether. It is also important to be aware of the fact that 'the teacher only speaks once'. When an error is pointed out you should do your best to correct it and commit it to memory so that you do not perform the same mistake in front of them again, for to do so would be considered very bad manners and could leave the senior feeling that they have wasted their time on you. They may be less willing to help you in future!

The old style teacher student relationship allows no place for the student to hide. The attention of the teacher is solely upon the student and they will feel as though the teacher's eyes are burning through them as they perform their techniques. Kinjo Seikichi *sensei* shared a wonderful anecdote about his experiences of performing *kata* in front of Miyagi Chojun *sensei*. Every Tuesday evening the students of Miyagi *sensei's* garden *dojo* would perform *kata* in front of their teacher one by one. He said that Miyagi *sensei* would sit on a stool with his hands resting on his knees. He would sit directly in front of the student whilst they performed their *kata* alone and his strong gaze would remain upon them the whole time. If the *kata* was performed to Miyagi *sensei's* liking, he would simply grunt and nod his head once as an indication for the next student to take the floor. If something caught his sharp eye though, he would correct the student or have a *sempai* assist with the technical details. Kinjo *sensei* said that he was always very nervous performing *kata* in front of his teacher. After relaying this story Kinjo *sensei* then had us perform *kata* for him in the same manner. Needless to say, this was probably the most nervous I had ever been during *kata*! I am very thankful to Kinjo *sensei* for sharing this story and often think of it when I am practicing.

So please do not be too upset with yourself for not performing to the best of your ability in front of your teacher. Any good *sensei* will know exactly what you are going through, for they will have felt the same things in front of their own *sensei*. Instead you should be happy that you have the personal pride to want to give a good account of yourself and not let your teacher down. Take on board their advice following the performance and then work hard to absorb their observations so that next time you will do better. Always try your best; this is all that is required.

# Using The Kata

I was recently asked the question 'how can we make sure we understand them properly' in relation to *kata*. I found this question very interesting and it has been a topic of conversation between my *sensei* and I for quite a long time. I still find it difficult to answer this question definitively, and I have only my own working theories based on the various methods I have seen and practiced over the years, as well as my own practical experience of self-defense and how it relates to *karate* from the many situations which have arisen at work.

When it comes to analyzing a technique in order to discover its possible application, it can be very easy to lose sight of what you are actually trying to achieve. The whole point of *karate* is that when all other means of avoidance or escape are exhausted, you act decisively to extract yourself from a situation as quickly as possible. The key word here is decisive. Any application which is long winded, complicated, overly visually impressive or only capable of working for somebody who is young and physically strong is probably wrong. I'm not a big believer in making every technique a joint lock or nerve strike of some sorts, nor am I a fan of flow drills or multiple techniques stringed together into long sequences. In fact, I'm not a great advocate of drilling applications that much at all, but I do believe you should have a reason for every technique. I realize this may sound like a contradiction but some things are not able to be explained very well in words. Such is the nature of martial arts unfortunately.

From my experience, and from what I have seen occur with colleagues, this is what usually happens. A threat will present itself; you react instinctively with a gross motor skill, usually a punch to the general area of the face. The reaction of the opponent to that strike then determines what happens next; however, the first punch rarely results in finishing the opponent so then you close the range, seize the opponent and then take them to the ground where they can then be restrained. This basic format happens the vast majority of the time and follows the *'mittsu no horitsu'*, implying that the situation should be over within three movements. This is a good rule to apply to *kata*. The *kata* part for me usually happens after the first strike, when I then seize the opponent and perform a technique depending upon the circumstances presented at that point to then put them to the ground. You see, as soon as you have a contact point with the opponent you are performing *kakie*. *Kakie* is the link between *kata* and *Jissen*.

What is interesting to me is my first instinctive reaction. I spend time every day striking the *machiwara* with *chudan tsuki*, aiming for the *ganka* point on the opponent which is located in the depression in between the ribs just below the nipple. Every day I perform *Sanchin* a number of times, also aiming the punches at the *ganka* point. I regularly perform *Sanseiru*, *Seisan* and *Suparinpei* more than any other *kata*, for these are my favorites, again aiming my punches at the *ganka* point during the opening three punches. So, my first instinctive reaction is to strike the opponent where? *Ganka* right? No, every time, my training goes out of the window and I hit any random target on the head without ever taking a deliberate aimed shot. How many times do we use *jodan tsuki* in the *kata* of *Goju Ryu*? *Gekisai*, this is the only time. So why do I always do this? It is very frustrating and almost impossible for me to override. I don't know if this is a problem which is peculiar to me, but if it is something which happens to many people, what is the point of having lots of elaborate *bunkai* if it seems whenever a need arises for us to defend ourselves, we resort to gross motor skills and whatever occurs naturally? I wonder whether this was at the forefront of Higashionna *sensei's* mind when he changed *Sanchin* to incorporate the closed fists rather than *nukite*?

What is very encouraging though, is what happens after the initial (usually ineffective) strike. After a rushed first response, the distance is closed either by the opponent reacting naturally by grabbing at you to keep their balance following being hit, or as they stagger back, you rush forward to close the distance and take hold of them, moving off toward the outer gate as in *kakie*. Any technique I have ever used within this range has come straight from *kata*, and the interesting thing is this; rarely is it an application which I have drilled with a training partner. Through practicing the various *kata* of *Goju Ryu* over and over, my body has learnt to move in a certain way in response to a movement which is either forced by the opponent, or due to my body position in relation to the opponent. For example, I was once in a confined area with a man and upon searching the waistband of his trousers, I found a knife. The male immediately began reaching for the knife so I grabbed his wrists to prevent this, pulling them to the side of my body, away from his weapon. With my hands 'tied up' I instinctively drove my body toward him at a 45 degree angle using a shoulder bump into his sternum to unbalance him and weaken his posture. With his structure then broken from this initial action I followed up with a head-butt to his face and removed the weapon from reach. Following this incident I conducted my own 'de-brief', which I always do, walking through the incident in slow time, alone in the *dojo*. I perform the exact techniques I used, just like a *kata*, and I 'feel' the movements, looking for a link between my instinctive reaction and the *kata*. On this occasion the movement felt the same as *Shisochin* where you move off at a 45 degree angle prior to the arm bar. It doesn't mean that this is the application for that particular technique; it just means this is how the *kata* served me during that set of particular circumstances which will probably never happen again in exactly the same way. This unpredictability of a live situation is what negates the need to memorize 100's of pre-determined responses to attacks which will probably never happen. Luckily enough, the *kata* has already remembered every response you will ever need; you just have to trust in them and invest the time to absorb the movements so that they become natural habits.

To best prepare yourself for self-defense, I think the following are the most important aspects from a *Goju Ryu* perspective;

**Kata** - Practice, practice, practice and absorb! You must move beyond the 'memory test' stage of performing so that the movements can just happen. Only then can the mind be free to concentrate upon the correct visualization, imagery and the production of the necessary emotional content and mental attributes necessary for the *kata* to become live.

**Condition the tools** – The various strikes of *kata* are worthless if the tool is not as strong as its delivery. If you strike harder than the tool you are using is capable of absorbing, this will most likely result in injury to yourself. Each tool must be conditioned to the extent that you can deliver the necessary force required to have the desired effect upon the opponent without damaging yourself. An understanding of human anatomy and the weak areas of the body is also vital.

**Kakie** – This exercise promotes the ability to maintain and disrupt correct body structure and alignment whilst also providing the bridge between *kata* application and *jissen* through the practice of *kakie dameshi*.

If these three areas are combined with the correct mindset, *Goju Ryu* will emerge in your responses.

Going back to my *jodan tsuki* problem briefly, luckily this is something which probably won't apply to 90% of the people practicing *Goju Ryu*. Unless you are a law enforcement officer or working in the security and protection industry, the likelihood of you having to deliver a pre-emptive strike is fairly remote. It is far more likely that if you are forced to defend yourself you will already be under attack and because of this, will already be in *kakie* range. I am assuming here that most people practicing *Goju Ryu* do not enjoy fighting and would do everything they could to avoid it. Allowing yourself to be placed in a position which would require a pre-emptive strike would either be due to a serious error in judgment, or an ego preventing you from backing down. Robbers will not give you the luxury of standing at punching range whilst using posturing and clever psychology to create an opportunity to take them out with a single punch.

This is their job! They work with 'shock and awe' tactics, overwhelming you with surprise, aggression and speed of approach to ensure that you don't have time to settle and plan a response. If you are attacked it will most likely be an ambush type scenario where you will be on the back foot from the start, this is where skill in *kakie* is essential.

*Kata* and *kakie* provide the tools required to get you out of a tight spot. In the clinch range where your arms are pinned, *kata* has the answer. Where your initial strike has failed and the opponent clings to your torso before attempting to tackle you to the ground, *kata* has the answer. Where your structure has been compromised and the opponent has managed to secure a headlock, *kata* has the answer. What *kata* doesn't address so directly are the instances where we have no contact point with the opponent, no link, no *kakie*. I think these are the circumstances where *mae geri* is particularly useful, and perhaps this is why Miyagi *sensei* was so keen upon incorporating the *mae geri* & *hiji ate* combination in the various different *kata*.[11] This technique in its many different forms provides an excellent method of closing the gap and attaining the close range favored in *Goju Ryu*.

*Kata* also contains a multitude of control and restraint techniques which are particularly useful to Law Enforcement Officers and those who work in the security and protection industry. It is very important to understand that the desired outcomes of Law Enforcement and Civilian self-defense are quite different. The primary goal of the civilian is to distract and escape, whereas the Police Officer may have to detain and arrest using reasonable force. Most of the time the suspect is not necessarily fighting the officer, but rather resisting against the officers' actions in order to escape arrest. This changes the threat levels and the amount of force which is reasonable to be used in such circumstances, and makes it necessary to employ the control and restraint techniques of *kata* known as *karamidi*, *tuidi* and *kin'na*. Using limb entanglements, joint locks and the seizing of vulnerable areas, it becomes possible to immobilize an opponent and get them into a position from which they can be safely handcuffed. Such methods are not particularly useful in civilian self-defense and may result in putting the defender in more danger than by simply disengaging from the opponent and running away. It is important to realize the difference and not become overly concerned with control and restraint as part of your training if your life circumstances do not deem it essential. *Karate* is primarily a striking art and *kata* concentrates its efforts upon facilitating an escape by using strikes to vulnerable targets on

---

[11] Interestingly the mae geri & hiji ate combination does not feature in Tou'on Ryu Sanseiru or Peichurin, leading me to believe this was an innovation of Miyagi sensei

the opponent. The applications you use in *kata* should reflect the circumstances you are more likely to find yourself in. But, if you are teaching *karate* to others, you should become familiar with such methods in case a student presents themselves who might require such skills or at least be prepared to recommend the student studies these particular skills from another source. This is how it was done in the old days where a student required certain things for their development which their own *sensei* thought beyond their particular expertise.

There are no secrets to *kata*, but there are a lot of right and wrongs. At what point does our personal interpretation of a movement stray from the purpose of the *kata* and become something of our own invention? This is a very difficult question to answer because *kata* should be very individual and subjective, but if a technique is long winded, complicated, relies on fine motor skills and dexterity, or is dependent upon the opponent reacting in a certain way, it is probably wrong. One thing is for sure; the opponent will never do what you expect, so don't allow your applications to rely upon their reactions. The whole 'I do this, which makes him do that, then he strikes me here so I block it and counter here which makes him do this' approach is pure fantasy and entirely pointless. The human body does have a number of natural responses to certain triggers, but we shouldn't rely upon these because, certainly in the case of persons under the influence of illegal drugs or those suffering from mental illness, such responses do not always occur, and their pain threshold is often much higher than an average person. On occasions they simply won't notice what you are doing and will continue to attack you regardless of any clever feints or techniques intended to illicit a pain withdrawal reflex.

When it comes to deciphering the application, always ask 'am I following the movement of the *kata*?' and 'does my application adhere to the principle being implied?' Do not try to force a square peg into a round hole in order to make your application fit a movement. The *kata* are quite logical and if it feels wrong or awkward, your application is probably incorrect (assuming you have sufficiently absorbed the *kata* of course). Most things in *kata* are hidden in plain sight and do not require any modification of the movements in order to make the application work. The only things which might change are the target areas depending upon the size of the performer and the position of the opponent; the actual movements remain the same.

It is my honest held belief that the solo practice of *kata* should form the bulk of the training in *karate*. All other areas of practice are conducted in order to enhance the *kata* by adding feeling and intent through experience. *Karate* is self-taught in that the information is laid out plainly before you, but how well you can use this is largely dependent upon the amount of time you are prepared to dedicate to absorbing the postures and movements so that they can occur spontaneously without conscious thought. Once this has been achieved, the applications will reveal themselves depending upon the individual circumstances presented at a given moment. The difficult part for many is having the faith that this will happen.

**Barrett sensei practicing** *kata*

# Balanced Training

I genuinely love being in the *dojo*. Even on those days (yes I get them too!) where the last thing I really feel like doing is training, once I step foot inside I am rewarded with a feeling that I cannot seem to get elsewhere. For me it is the chance of having a few moments where there are no outside distractions that is most welcome; an opportunity to listen and get to know myself.

Much is written about the benefits of meditation, and there are many *karateka* who incorporate such practices within their *dojo*. Aside from a couple of minute's *zazen* at the beginning and end of our group training sessions, meditation is not something that I practice. It's not that I do not find it useful or enjoyable; it's just that I believe I am able to get the same benefits from my regular *karate* training without having to devote extra time to meditation which could be better served elsewhere in my study.

Once we pass through the 'memory test' period of training where the majority of our thoughts relate to 'what technique comes next?' or 'is my arm in the right position?' we can either choose to direct our minds toward achieving specific tasks, or simply allow them to wander and see where our thoughts take us.

I personally like to vary my own practice between hard sessions which are conducted in silence, and more experimental sessions where I will play some classical Okinawan, Japanese or Chinese music quietly in the background while I train. Both approaches have their benefits.

For the hard sessions I believe it is important that there be minimal distractions so that you can really listen to what is going on inside your head. It is quite common to see world class athletes training to music which they find inspirational, with a tempo suited to picking them up when their bodies start to fatigue. For *karate* though I think all the work should come from the individual without help from any outside sources. When met with hardship in life you cannot rely upon having a heavy rock or rap soundtrack with motivational lyrics to spur you on, nor your friends in your corner shouting for you to keep going and not give up. All of this must come from inside your own heart. No distractions means there is nowhere for your mind to go, nowhere to hide, and your every thought is directed straight back at you. When it starts to hurt, your mind will tell you it hurts; there is no escaping these thoughts and feelings. How you deal with them though is the important part. Training under such circumstances teaches you to trust yourself and you develop a quiet determination to grit your teeth and push through whatever challenges you are faced with. At first when you tell yourself to perform 'one more, one more, you can do this' it can be difficult to believe in yourself and you may think it is beyond your physical capabilities; however, the more you do this and succeed, the more you can listen to your own positive encouragement and take strength from it. The body is capable of far more than we realize and the stronger you can make your spirit and your will to succeed, the better your body will respond to what you are asking from it. Set your targets high and don't stop until you smash through them. On the occasions when you are successful in reaching your goals, you can be proud that you did it all yourself.

It is through hard training that we can really develop an understanding of who we actually are, and the thoughts that present themselves under such circumstances are some of the most honest ones we will ever have,

untainted by opinion or desire. This is what I mean by a conversation with the self. Through austere training we come into contact with our true nature, and often our grand illusions of ourselves are completely shattered when met with the reality of the moment. The rebuilding phase that follows is what dictates how we will grow and evolve, or whether we will continue to stay still and avoid such challenges in the future. To come out of the other end of hardship is a great achievement, but to then face it again and again with full knowledge of what it entails is a different thing altogether.

For the more experimental practice sessions where I am searching for fresh ideas and different approaches to familiar themes, I enjoy listening to Okinawan music. I believe this to be the soundtrack of *karate*, and I am always filled with fond memories of Okinawa, especially when the sun is shining outside on a warm day. The music on these occasions prevents my mind from wandering too far from the task at hand. The odd thought of 'what shall I eat for lunch today?' can be quickly banished away and put off until later while I listen to the unhurried rhythm of the *Sanshin* and feel for the connections between the various techniques and exercises as I work through my *kata*. I have long had a problem in my *karate* in that I am too rigid in both mind and technique, and my *kata* is sometimes rushed and forced. The relaxing sound of the *Sanshin* allows me to rid my mind of excess tension and simply enjoy the movements of *karate* while I work toward softening my techniques and developing a fluidity and balance to my *kata*. The different rhythms within the music remind me that *kata* is a living thing with a tempo suited to the particular circumstances that the various techniques address. Performing a slow technique fast, or vice versa, invalidates many of the applications and it is important to perform each movement with the required levels of *Go* or *Ju* so that they remain at their most effective. Sports *kata* has an unnatural rhythm which does not relate to self-defense. True *kata*, like nature, has a balanced yet unpredictable rhythm which changes according to the conditions. A regular rhythm is easy to detect and upset, but it is very difficult to understand the timing of falling raindrops. This is nature's rhythm which is irregular, and nature still regularly catches us all off guard despite our advances in technology. This unpredictability is what we should aim for when faced with an opponent. Modern music has set rhythms which are regular and easy to dance to but classical music has peaks and falls, fast and slow sections, and parts which are heavy or light. I think this is more similar to our classical *kata*. Classical Chinese and Japanese music mimics the sounds of nature closely so I think this kind of music is a good accompaniment to *karate* training. I like to conduct these training sessions in the early morning before the activities of the day have allowed my mind to collect clutter. By avoiding TV, internet, newspapers and radio before my morning training, I can devote my full attention to *karate* and allow ideas to spontaneously evolve under their own momentum without having to force them too much. These are some of my most rewarding sessions and I am regularly surprised at how *karate* continues to reveal more of itself as I look deeper.

The two different approaches to personal training which I have described above complement each other very well as a way of *Go* and *Ju*. You should balance your training accordingly to have both sufficient personal challenge as well as enough opportunity for technical growth and development as a way of working toward the unification of *Shin, Gi, Tai*. I have in the past devoted too much time to hard training and not enough to recovery and technical development, and this imbalance revealed itself in both my technique and personality. I approach my training in a more natural way these days and I have found that the results are far superior to my previous efforts, even though on occasions it feels as though I am not trying as hard. Modern approaches to sports science and the training of elite athletes recognize the need for balance between *Go* and *Ju*, as do the fields of academics and the arts. *Karate* contains a good balance of hard and soft, but it is essential that we do not emphasize one over the other, and contribute equally to both aspects.

# The Performance of Kata

**Okinawan Karate** shares common roots with *Silat*

I'm very sorry to admit this, but I find most *kata* performances very boring to watch. This is particularly true of *Goju Ryu* because I am more familiar with the *kata* of this school so there isn't even the mystery of what happens next in the sequence. But, there are certain people who really make me sit up and take notice. They do not have any special interpretation of the movements, no added dramatics, no stage presence or anything like that; on the contrary their executions of the *kata* are usually quite humble and stripped bare of any of the nonsense which seems to be wrapped around *karate* these days. Well, the ones I prefer are anyway...

There can be no denying that, on the surface, many of the top level *kata* competitors in sports *karate* have almost perfect looking techniques. Their postures are precise, their athleticism impressive, and they have great speed which links together the individual movements in a staccato like rhythm, showing the picture perfect end positions of each technique very nicely. But despite all of this, there is something missing. Something quite big which makes me lose interest the moment they step foot on the mat, before the first technique has even begun. I think it is honesty.

I have been very lucky to have had the opportunity to travel around Thailand, Malaysia and Indonesia and witness how their native martial traditions are practiced, and what impressed me the most about their approach was the honesty about it. *Muay Thai* gyms consisted of a small space between buildings with a corrugated metal sheet bridging the gap to act as a makeshift roof while the fighters performed sit-ups in the road outside. *Silat* was practiced barefoot in a jungle clearing with the practitioners stripped to the waist in their normal daily attire while they trained. It made me think about how similar this was to how *karate* training was conducted in the not so distant past. It seems a million years apart from what often passes as *dojo* today. The demonstrations I witnessed were dirty and raw, with the practitioners doing it for nobody but themselves. It was very honest and very humbling.

The moment you are more concerned about how your performance appears to somebody watching rather than what you are feeling in yourself, you have lost it. If you are doing the *kata* correctly there simply isn't time to worry about how you look to an observer, your mind is already fully occupied on more important things. If the correct mindset is adopted, this will reveal itself in every movement of the performer, and this is exciting to watch. To see any craftsman fully committed to the task at hand is inspiring.

*Kata* is comprised of a sequence of movements which contain both hard and soft elements. An understanding of each is necessary to bring the *kata* to life. One of my major concerns with sports *kata* is that the rhythm and timing is unrealistic and has no relation to the actual application of the techniques. I find Miyazato *sensei's* comment quite amusing where he says 'sometimes the performers pause for so long that I think they've forgotten the next movement.'[12]

In the *kata* of Goju Ryu there are parts where there are deliberate pauses within the sequence of movements. These are not for dramatic effect, but to ensure that the technique stands a better chance of hitting the target. An example of this is the *hiza geri* & *mae geri* combination in *Saifa*. Both kicks are performed from the same leg without returning it to the ground. It is now common to see both techniques being performed quickly one after the other, but in the *Jundokan* the correct method was to pause briefly after the *hiza geri*. This allows time for the opponent's body to react to the strike which then opens up the next target. If the *mae geri* is delivered too quickly, the *ma'ai* is incorrect and the kick is less effective. When you strike somebody in the groin, there is often a delayed reaction

---

[12] The Last Interview DVD – Jundokan (www.okinawadirect.com)

and the opponent's body will bend forward at the waist before staggering a couple of paces backward. *Saifa* takes this into account and this is why there is a pause at this point. This kind of thing happens frequently elsewhere within the classical *kata* of *Goju Ryu*. The moment that the timing is changed for visual effect, the movement is rendered less effective. When modified versions of the techniques are then taught, the original effective versions of *kata* become lost to time. Regrettably this has already been happening for many years, even during the days of Miyagi Chojun *sensei*. Frequently during my times in Okinawa I have been told 'the old way of performing this technique was like this, but it was changed because it was too difficult'. These changes, I was informed, were made during the days of Miyagi *sensei* and came as a result of significant pressure from the Japanese to make *karate* more acceptable on the mainland. Desperate to see the art he loved acknowledged with the same level of respect afforded to *Judo* and *Kendo*, Miyagi *sensei* was forced to concede on certain technical issues it would appear. If this is true, I think it is a great shame. Before we blame Miyagi *sensei* too much though, it is important to understand that there was a significant amount of prejudice against the Okinawan people from the mainland Japanese during this period. Proud of his roots and fellow countrymen, Miyagi *sensei* saw *karate* as a means of promoting Okinawan culture and made such changes with the best intentions.

By developing a good understanding of the possibilities available in every technique of *kata*, the correct way to perform the movements becomes apparent. Techniques where you grasp an opponent to pull them off balance before striking require you to first be in a stable, rooted posture, before using heavy *muchimi* in order to establish *kazushi*. The timing of this cannot be rushed, or too slow. The same applies to the various *kansetsu waza*; a rushed technique will cause you to lose contact with the opponent's limb, making the attack ineffective. The movements of *kata* are performed in a certain manner for a good reason. Once we think we know better and begin changing the tempo of the techniques to be 'more realistic' or 'more impressive' we lose a significant portion of the information that is available to us and to future generations who will go on to learn our new modified versions of the *kata*. This would be most unfortunate.

Just as you wouldn't add your own brush strokes to a Da Vinci masterpiece, the classical *kata* should not be tainted by our own personal approaches when it comes to teaching. The *kata* have their origins in antiquity and are ours to possess for only a short time. Because of this, it cannot be considered that we ever truly own the *kata* for we are only borrowing them briefly; looking after them carefully until the next generation has their turn. The *kata* transcend time and are the way our ancestors communicate their ideas and experiences with us. In an art where we are cursed with a lack of written documentation from the past, we should view the *kata* as *karate's* legacy and respect them accordingly.

**There is a raw honesty about how training used to be conducted**

# The Cycle Of The Sun & Moon

*Ketsumyaku wa nichigetsu ni nitari*

*The circulatory rhythm of the body is similar to the cycle of the sun and the moon*

This short phrase found in the *Bubishi* is very cryptic I think, and it is something which has given me lots to consider over the years. I quite enjoy solving puzzles and this is why I like *Goju Ryu* so much. The whole art from its early history to its *kata* and training methods is very mysterious and contains enough to keep a person searching for answers for an entire lifetime. With regards to the above phrase, I do not think I am yet close to fully solving this riddle, but I do have some ideas for now which I can research further as time goes on.

For this article I would like to discuss an issue related to timing rather than focusing too much on the diurnal cycle described elsewhere in the *bubishi*, for this is covered in some depth by Mr McCarthy in his excellent translation and commentary of the work.

Our planet is constantly turning about the sun whilst the moon is simultaneously cycling around the earth. The lunar cycle takes approximately 29.5 days, whereas the rotation of the earth around the sun takes 365+ days. From this, it is easy to see that there is a great difference in timing between the circulations of the sun and the moon. I wonder if this coincides with the Small Circulation and Grand Circulation in *Qigong*?

The Small Circulation focuses upon the movement of *Qi* around the Conception and Governing Meridians, whereas the Grand Circulation includes moving *Qi* around the limbs and extremities of the body. Naturally the Grand Circulation is a longer process than the Small. In untrained people the whole process of moving Qi around the Grand Circulation is believed to occur naturally over 365 days, whereas one full cycle of the Small Circulation is thought to happen once every 24 hours. Does the Sun relate to the Grand Circulation and the Moon to the Small Circulation? In *Qigong* it is believed that a person can speed up these natural processes through training so that they are able to occur within a single cycle of breath through awakening the *tanden* and increasing the rate at which energy is circulated along the Governing and Conception meridians. This is one of the advanced training practices of *Sanchin*. The rapid breathing method at the end of the *kata* encourages the *tanden* to condense and rotate at an ever increasing pace before releasing suddenly and returning to its natural state. This is a very difficult thing to correctly describe with words and is something which needs to be felt and experienced to be properly appreciated.

A 24 hour day is also divided into periods relating to *Yin* and *Yang*. Midnight is Strong *Yin*, 6am is Weakening *Yin* / Growing *Yang*. 12pm is Strong *Yang*, 6pm is Weakening *Yang* / Growing *Yin*. In basic terms night is *Yin*, day is *Yang*. Furthermore, each two hour segment of a 24 hour day is associated with either *Yin* or *Yang* according to the Diurnal Cycle as *Qi* circulates around the 12 main meridians. The former theory relating to the changing of *Yin* and *Yang* over a 24 hour period can be likened to the Solar cycle, whereas the latter theory relating to Diurnal Cycle would represent the Lunar cycle.

In relation to the *Bubishi* I find these theories quite intriguing as they open up different possibilities to what is usually attributed to this short phrase. Due to a significant portion of the *bubishi* being dedicated to the study of vital points, the most obvious way of interpreting the phrase *Ketsumyaku wa nichigetsu ni nitari* is to associate it with the principles of striking vulnerable points. This may well be true, but much of the *bubishi* also concerns matters relating to medicine and health. I wonder whether this phrase relates to matters of health promotion as well as martial application. A clever blend of *Go* and *Ju* hidden within a single sentence. There appears to be a lot which is bubbling away underneath the surface of the obvious when it comes to this phrase. Like *kata*, the more we investigate such things, the more we can gain from them to better enhance our understanding.

The *Kenpo Hakku*, in which this phrase is written, is a general set of principles which cover a wide variety of subjects rather than focusing solely upon martial aspects. It appears to be almost like a *dojo kun*, providing an overview of *Kenpo* ranging from tactics, strategies and mindset, to the promotion of general health. It is little wonder that Miyagi *sensei* considered the text *'the bible of karatedo'*. Every time I read the *Bubishi* I am rewarded with something new which I hadn't noticed previously. There can be no doubt that this is the single most important text relating to *Goju Ryu*, and all serious students should refer to it frequently.

# Leave Things Better

Every year in April and October our group holds *Gasshuku* to commemorate the dates of Miyagi Chojun *sensei's* birth and passing. These are great opportunities for everybody to immerse themselves in their training, and the shared experiences help to forge strong relationships outside of the *dojo*, promoting a family like atmosphere amongst the members. Much thought goes into the planning of these events by my teacher Richard Barrett *sensei* who always manages to fit a few unexpected surprises into the schedule.

At our 10 year anniversary *Gasshuku* in October 2011, we were awoken long before dawn to drive to a beach for our morning training session. Standing in a circle we bowed in as a group, and then began to work our way through Miyagi *sensei's junbi undo* together. With the rare luxury of space afforded through being outside of the *dojo*, conducting group training whilst stood in a circle was a nice idea which was promoted by Kinjo Seikichi *sensei*. In his typically humble manner he explained to us that he preferred teaching like this as he didn't like standing out in front telling people what to do. Training in a circle helped make him feel more involved and closer to the students. As we trained in this manner I thought about Kinjo *sensei* and once again hoped that I could follow his example of what a *karateka* could be.

Following *junbi undo* we turned as a group to face the sun as it appeared over the horizon of the ocean, transforming the sky into a beautiful assortment of colours whilst we performed *Sanchin*. Small relatively unimportant training sessions such as these are the ones I often find my mind thinking back to, reliving the experiences and enjoying the moment again and again. There is something very natural about practicing *karate* on a beach at dawn, and no matter where I go in the world, this is something I always try to do. I've absolutely no doubt that there are many *karateka* all over the world that also enjoy doing the same thing, and I feel a certain kinship with them through this shared experience.

Our morning training continued on, and with the group suitably exhausted by the end of it, we sat on the sand to dry off and enjoy breakfast together. Barrett *sensei* walked off to collect a few items from his car, and returned a short while later with some trash bags. He explained that because we had borrowed the beach for our training that morning we should do something in return to leave our practice area in a better condition than it was originally found. We split into groups of two and then walked the length of the beach, picking up any trash that had been discarded onto the beach, and in no time we had all filled our bags, ensuring all that remained on the sand were our footprints.

This small gesture did not take long to perform and all that was required were a few trash bags and a willingness to do something good for other people. Acts such as this are very important in *karate*. It is good for the soul, good for the ego, good for the environment, and good for forging bonds between students through a shared task. Things like this are often overlooked these days, and not just in *karate* either.

I have been extremely fortunate in the short time I have been practicing to have met so many good examples of *karateka*. They are not especially memorable for their technical ability, knowledge of *karate*, strength as a fighter or anything like that; for me the thing I enjoy seeing most is how they interact with other people and their local communities. My various seniors have had me doing all kinds of things such as moving washing machines, helping at a senior citizens exercise group, cutting down trees, washing toilets, carrying a drunk person home, building walls, digging out caves, painting stuff, sanding stuff, digging stuff, sawing stuff, and all kinds of other stuff. Friends of mine often joke with me about the Karate Kid movies, but I always tell them that the original film actually wasn't too far from the truth!

Hokama *sensei* once told me that 'a *karateka* should have a positive influence on the people around them'. I think this is a very desirable ability to seek through our training.

Just like we borrowed the beach for our morning training session, we can only ever borrow *karatedo* for the relatively short duration of our lifespan. It is important that we take great care to leave the art in a better condition than when we accepted control of it so that it remains intact for future generations to enjoy. This too includes elements of trash clearing, because many of *karate's* users have not been very careful and we seem to have collected a lot of garbage along the way which now ruins the appearance of the art. This is no problem so long as we accept responsibility and do what we can to clean up, however; if we also continue to accumulate trash over the coming years, pretty soon the art will be buried so deep that nobody will even notice it is there.

The trash bag is over there so what are you waiting for? Get started!

# **A Zen Experience**

Some years ago, I was fortunate enough to have an opportunity to attend the *Kozenji* in Shuri for morning *zazen* practice. The *Zen* Center is situated on the slope of Shuri Castle, at the top of the Kinjo stone pavement, and is run by Sakiyama Sogen *Roshi* who was a former *karate* student of Miyagi Chojun *sensei* as a young man.

I arrived at Shuri Castle before sunrise and enjoyed walking around the grounds for a little while, making the most of being away from the crowds that gathered there during the day. I find this provides a much better opportunity to soak in the atmosphere and walk the same ground as the famous *Bushi* of the Ryukyu Kingdom. There are also some great views of Naha from the vantage point of the castle which are best appreciated at night. Under the moonlight I could make out the silhouettes of bats flying overhead, their silent gliding above providing an eerie setting for the morning's activities as I made my way back toward the entrance of the Zen Center.

A lone monk beat a wooden board rhythmically, breaking the mornings silence to indicate that it was now time to enter. Walking past him into the large reception area I removed my shoes before stepping onto the *tatami*. I was delighted to see that Higaonna Morio *sensei* was also in attendance, dressed in a simple dark *kimono* and *hakama*. In the main meditation room I found my spot and arranged my cushions to make myself as comfortable as possible, and following this I struggled to bend my legs into a half lotus position, which for me was no easy task. I would remain in this position for the next hour, with a short break halfway through to stretch my legs and get some blood back into them.

If for any moment I thought that sitting and doing nothing for an hour would be an easy or relaxing task, my illusion was about to be shattered completely. What followed was one of the most difficult challenges I'd ever had, both physically and mentally; comparable to the toughest *karate* training sessions that I had experienced. Not being blessed with the greatest of flexibility, the half lotus position became quite painful very early into the session. Not wanting to disturb the other practitioners by shuffling about to change position, I would have to endure this pain silently and wait until the end before I could move my legs again. My whole body was shaking with pain and I tried my best to block this out by allowing my mind to wander with the sounding of the chimes and bells, the smell of the incense, and the view of the magnificent sunrise over the hills of Shuri. My practice session became an exercise of acceptance and endurance. Acceptance of the fact that I was stuck there for the foreseeable future, and there was nothing I could do about it, so I had no choice but to endure and push through. As I had found during hard training in my *karate*, following such acceptance things become much easier. You stop feeling sorry for yourself and just get on with it. This is a very useful quality to be able to possess I think. Over the course of the practice session I would experience exactly the same feelings, thoughts, fears and doubts that I was required to face in the *dojo*. I was quite amazed at how this could be accomplished simply through sitting quietly.

The bell that was struck at various points of the session reverberated around the room and seemed to come from all directions at once; it was a really wonderful sound. As my body began to settle and become more accustomed to the position that I was sat, I began to enjoy my surroundings a lot more and worked on settling my mind and breathing to occur correctly from the *tanden*.

A solitary monk walked silently up and down the line holding a long wooden stick which he would occasionally strike down onto the shoulders of a willing practitioner. As he stopped in front of me, I bowed toward him and lowered my head to present my shoulders. With the wooden stick he struck down twice sharply onto each shoulder before moving off again to help the next person. These slaps, although painful, were also very invigorating and helped to 'wake up' the body and mind. I was struck (quite literally!) by the similarity to *shime* in *Sanchin* training.

The bell struck one final time to signal the end of practice and everyone tidied up the area they had been sat in. Luckily for me, Sakiyama *Roshi* had agreed to give a lecture about the relationship between *zazen* and *karate* in the downstairs classroom area with Higaonna *sensei*. I rubbed some life back into my aching legs and settled down comfortably with my notebook to enjoy the lecture which focused upon *Sanchin*. Sakiyama *Roshi* explained that the outcome of a battle was dependent upon who could keep their hips forward, and who is able to maintain good posture and balance. Having a strong *tanden* enables a person to be like a *Dharuma* doll. No matter what direction the doll is pushed, it always springs upright again; this is the correct attitude for *budo*. The *tanden* itself does not relate to the point two inches below the navel, but is actually an area which is found inside a triangle formed between three points, consisting of the navel, the pubic bone and the point on the spine which is directly in line with the navel.

Sakiyama *Roshi* explained the purpose of the strikes onto the shoulders with the wooden stick during *zazen* as not being as a form of punishment, but rather a way of assisting the practitioner with realizing their human potential. Like in *Sanchin*, as the body fatigues the mind begins to wander and lose concentration. Once this occurs, everything becomes more difficult. In *Sanchin* we receive slaps onto the shoulders which serve to invigorate the body and encourage martial spirit. In *zazen* it is the same. The strikes awaken weary bodies and minds, and help to summon 'human power' from the *tanden*. Sakiyama *Roshi* explained that every person is born with the potential to become great. The source of this potential is the 'human power' which resides in the *tanden*.

Sakiyama *Roshi* was 82 years old when I met him on this occasion and he said that he fondly remembered his training with Miyagi *sensei* and respected him very much. Every morning Sakiyama *Roshi* would practice *Sanchin* and *Tensho* whilst lying in his bed before getting up. He attributed his good health to this daily routine.

**Bengadake in Shuri where Funakoshi Gichin *sensei* would often visit in order to reflect upon life**

# Busaganashi

The famous *Busaganashi* sculpture which stands in the *Jundokan dojo* is a very impressive work of art which once belonged to Miyagi Chojun *sensei*. This statue has fascinated me ever since my childhood and I am always excited to learn a little bit more about it, although detailed information is often difficult to find.

*Busaganashi* is the Okinawan name for the Chinese deity *Jiu Tian Feng Huo Yuan San Dou* which appears in the *Bubishi*.[13] According to Chinen Teruo *sensei*, during Miyagi *sensei's* first visit to Fuzhou China he saw many images of *Busaganashi*, and learnt that he was considered a local hero.[14] This was not just amongst martial artists though, for representations of him could also be found in many other settings such as shops, restaurants and family homes. Miyagi *sensei* returned to Okinawa with an image of *Busagashi* which he would continue to revere in his personal practice, devoting every 1st and 15th day to the deity.[15] Kinjo Seikichi *sensei* remembered there being special training sessions on these dates where all the students of the garden *dojo* would sit in a large circle where upon one at a time, they would then perform the various *kata* of *Goju Ryu* in front of Miyagi *sensei* and the rest of the group. He remembered that these were always very happy occasions for everybody involved. Once, during a large seminar for the 50th anniversary of the *Jundokan* in Okinawa, Kinjo *sensei* had everybody perform in this manner and I remember how happy he was to be continuing this tradition. I had to perform *Saifa* for him, and this *kata* now always reminds me of this nice memory.

A few years ago I was visiting my *sensei* in Spain when he presented me with my own wooden *Busaganashi* which he got carved locally by a man who made 3D jigsaw puzzles. It's a really unique piece of work which now stands proudly on the *Kamiza* in my *dojo*. I try my best to preserve Miyagi *sensei's* tradition of devoting the 1st and 15th of the month to *Busaganshi* by having the students replace the water and cuttings from the Bay Tree outside which are then placed in small vases which stand either side of the statue. These vases were bought in Tsuboya near to where Miyagi *sensei's* garden *dojo* once stood. I also light a candle on the *Kamiza*. This tradition in my *dojo* is not an act of worship, for I am not religious in the slightest, but rather a way of preserving a piece of information about

---

[13] Bubishi: The Bible of Karate, McCarthy, p71

[14] Forty Years of Chamber, Chinen, p26

[15] The History of Karate, Higaonna, p64

Miyagi *sensei* which might otherwise be lost to the sands of time. Although fairly small, and arguably trivial, this piece of information for me suggests a different side to Miyagi *sensei*. The various stories relating to him often focus on how severe his teaching was and how his students would be afraid of him, but the account given by Kinjo *sensei* suggests a happy family type atmosphere on these occasions where everybody would gather and enjoy *karate* together. I think this is something to be celebrated and preserved.

*Busaganshi* was respected due to his values of propriety, righteousness, virtue and perseverance, as well as his skill in the martial arts which is what enabled him to display and use these qualities in order to protect the people who relied upon him. He was the role model for all aspiring *Bushi*, the mythical master who they would hope to one day emulate. These days we are often impressed by the physical skills of the person, but sometimes forget to consider their character before we say how great they are. Remember *'no matter how you excel in the art of Te and your scholastic endeavors, nothing is more important than your behavior and your humanity as observed in everyday life'*.

We are now approaching the 100 year mark from when Miyagi *sensei* first learned about *Busaganashi* during his visit to Fuzhou. I hope that people will continue to look at the statue which stands in the *Jundokan* and consider what it represents, rather than thinking how cool it would look on an association badge or t-shirt. Why was Miyagi *sensei* so interested in *Busaganishi* in the first place?

**Busaganashi in the authors Uraniwa dojo**

# Karatedo & Healing

Martial arts and medicine were historically often taught together as part of a well-balanced system, but this has been largely neglected with the relative ease at which we can now receive medical attention. In ancient times it was common for people to die as a result of injuries sustained through combat, but this was not necessarily due to the martial arts being any more deadly back then, it was more to do with how regular people often couldn't afford to get their injuries treated. Because of this, open wounds would become infected, particularly in tropical climates. Broken bones would be left to heal on their own, and internal bleeds would go untreated, leading to a slow, painful death. These kinds of things are what inspired the stories surrounding the mysterious delayed death touch which is mentioned frequently in the *Bubishi*. Thankfully such problems are largely redundant for the majority of us these days, but a little knowledge about the healing arts can be extremely beneficial and an interesting adjunct to physical training.

Common sense would suggest that if you are regularly engaging in combat, whether real or simulated, there is a good chance that you will suffer from the occasional injury. A little knowledge about how to treat such injuries in their early stages can drastically shorten the amount of recovery time needed for the body to heal, and in more severe cases, an understanding of basic first aid can mean the difference between life and death for you, your training partner, or an opponent. Skill at dealing with cuts, sprains, strains, the treatment of shock and clearing airways is also extremely useful around the household and would benefit one's family greatly.

It is said that Higashionna Kanryo *sensei* was skilled not only in *toudi*, but also Chinese weaponry and medicine. It is interesting that his knowledge about these subjects appears not to have been passed on to any of his students. Higashionna *sensei* was not alone amongst practitioners of this era though, for it is known that Uechi Kanbun and Matayoshi Shinko also had a working knowledge of Chinese herbal medicine. Of course, the *bubishi* also devotes a significant amount of the text to the treatment of martial arts related injuries. Hokama *sensei* told me that many of the formulas and treatments contained within the *bubishi* relate more to injuries sustained through warfare rather than hand to hand fighting and that most likely the herbal treatments of the *bubishi* concerned the treatment of injuries sustained from weapons, ballistic trauma or falling from a horse, etc. Hokama *sensei* also told me that he received instruction in acupuncture and herbal medicine from his teachers Higa Seko *sensei* and

Fukuchi Seiko *sensei*. Whilst out walking together, Hokama *sensei* would regularly pause to point out different plants, roots or flowers which could be used in the treatment of various ailments ranging from the treatment of an eye contusion right through to maintaining sexual virility into old age.

Miyazato Eiichi *sensei* was asked in an interview whether Miyagi Chojun *sensei* practiced Chinese medicine, but he replied that he did not. Despite this, it would appear that Miyagi *sensei* was actually quite well respected within his local community with regards to first aid. Chinen Teruo *sensei* recalls an incident where his older brother dislocated his arm after falling from a tree. His mother immediately took him to Miyagi *sensei's dojo* where Miyagi was then able to put the arm back in place.[16] Of course, this does not suggest that Miyagi *sensei* was adept at Chinese medicine, but it does indicate that he at least had a working knowledge of basic injury management. It is my opinion that such things were common knowledge amongst many practitioners of that era. Motobu Choki for example presents information handed down through his family relating to the treatment of dislocations, broken bones, revival, cuts, swellings and herbal medicine in his 1926 publication *'Okinawa Kempo'*.

Of course, serious injuries will always require expert medical attention either at the hospital or from a doctor, but what we are discussing here are life preservation skills as taught in basic first aid, and the initial treatment of minor injuries which are received through training. It is essential, in my opinion, that every serious *karateka*, especially those teaching, should attend a course on basic first aid. This is the most important set of skills to possess with regard to treating a casualty. It is vital to think of the bigger picture regarding self-defense, and consider more than just the physical act of defending yourself from an attack. Knowing how to save your own life or that of a loved one in an emergency is a much more relevant skill for most people than being able to perform a fancy knife disarm.

I will present here some of the methods and remedies I personally use for common injuries which result from training. I have used these techniques to treat my own minor injuries in the past and have been impressed at the results. There is also some information relating to traditional revival techniques as passed on to me in Okinawa. The various methods described here are for the purpose of information only and should not be attempted without first consulting a qualified medical professional regarding the consequences of using such methods.

---

[16] Forty Years of Chamber, Chinen, p13

Kappo Jutsu

A basic guide to *Kappo Jutsu* was thoughtfully provided by Motobu Choki *sensei* in his 1926 book *'Okinawan Kempo'*. Widely regarded as one of the most experienced practitioners of his time in relation to actual combat through *kaki dameshi*, the fact that Motobu *sensei* balanced his confrontational nature with an apparently good understanding of how to heal is quite interesting. In addition to *Kappo Jutsu* methods, Motobu *sensei* also included various herbal formulas for treating injuries received through fighting.

Hokama *sensei* shared a little of his own understanding of *Kappo Jutsu* with me at his *dojo* in Nishihara. He explained that when a person is knocked unconscious as the result of a strike, they can be revived by positioning their legs so that the soles of their feet are touching. The soles of the feet can be considered to be similar to the + and − of an electrical circuit. When the soles of the feet are pressed together, they complete the circuit and provide a jolt of energy. The casualty should then be lifted into a seated position so that your shin presses against their spine, with you kneeling behind supporting their weight. From this position you then cup your hands underneath the casualty's armpits and pull their shoulders sharply backward whilst pressing your knee forward against their upper spine at the 9th vertebrate and shouting their name into their ear. This can also be accompanied by light slaps to the acupuncture point referred to as GB20 at the base of the skull. This method should be performed by two people, with one controlling the legs and the other controlling the upper body. Hokama *sensei* also described various solo methods as well as treatments for when a person is struck in the testicles or loses consciousness as a result of a choke or strangle.

For somebody who has been struck hard in the testicles, the pain can be relieved by having them jump up and down on the spot with their bodyweight landing in their heels. You then assist by slapping the palm of your hand hard into the small of their back and brushing your hand firmly downwards past their buttocks.

Detailed information relating to *Kappo Jutsu* is contained in Hokama *sensei's* English publication *'History and Traditions of Okinawan Karate'* and I would recommend for any person interested in learning more about this theory to consult this work as a starting point.

Martial Arts Injury Treatments

**Jow**: I am occasionally contacted regarding the use and effectiveness of *Jow* in relation to body conditioning and *machiwara* practice. I used to regularly use *Jow* both during and following my *machiwara* training, but to be perfectly honest I don't think it made any difference for me personally.

This isn't to say that *Jow* for such purposes is ineffective, but rather that in my own personal training I am quite careful with my use of the *machiwara*, and only do what my body is capable of performing on that particular day without becoming injured. There are various Iron Palm formulas and different types of *Jow* marketed specifically for *machiwara* use sold on the internet, and all of them are perfectly safe for external use, so there are lots of different options to experiment with in your own training.

I do however use two different types of *Jow* for the treatment of bruises, strains and sprains. As I mentioned, there are lots of different types of *Jow* available on the internet, and one of the most interesting companies is Shen (www.shenmartialarts.com) who specialize in Iron Body products and even have a *Jow* which is created from a formula reportedly used by Uechi Kanbun himself. There are a number of ready-made lotions as well as dried herbs which you can use to make your own if you require larger quantities. I have used products from Shen in the past and found them to be of good quality.

For my 30th birthday my wife kindly arranged for me to attend a course on Chinese herbal medicine for the treatment of martial arts related injuries with Mr Paul Robin, who is one of the UK's foremost authorities on Traditional Chinese Medicine. This was of course very interesting, but unfortunately much of the information was a little too far beyond my level of understanding for me to fully comprehend the amount of detail he was sharing. Despite this, I was able to learn how to create *Jow* in the form of lotions and balms. The herbs required to construct these formulas are easy enough to source, but can be quite expensive for the initial outlay so I would recommend getting ready-made dried herbs which work out much cheaper, but are generally of a slightly lower quality.

I have purposely left out the amount of each herb and omitted some of the key ingredients required to make this *Jow* in order to protect Mr Robin's recipe, and this list is presented for information purposes only to show the complexity of some of these formulas. A qualified TCM Doctor should be consulted before using any of the herbs listed below;

*Tao Re, Zhi Zi, Mo Yao, Ru Xiang, Xu Duan, Gu Sui Bu, San Qi, Sang Ji Sheng, Sang Zhi, Niu Xi, Hai Tong Pi, Wu Jia Pi, Wei Ling Xian, Qin Jiao, Su Mu, Bing Pia, Du Huo, Du Zhong, Gui Zhi, Mu Gua, Pu Huang, San Leng, Wang Bu Liu Xin, Xian Mao, Bei Xie, Tu Fu Ling, Huang Qin, Sang Shen, Hai Feng Ten, Yi Yi Ren.*

These herbs are grinded into a powder and then prepared using the following method, which can also be used for ready-prepared herbs;

Cook the herbs in Coconut Oil on a low setting (1 scoop of herbs to 4 scoops of oil). Allow to cool and then add a mix of 30% sesame oil, 30 %

hemp oil, 10 % jojoba oil, 5% camellia, and 5% wheat germ. Strain the oil though a muslin or similar cloth to remove any loose particles, and then transfer into bottles for storage.

The herbs can also be mixed into Vaseline (Petroleum Jelly) which is melted over a high setting in a ceramic slow cooker. The mixture can then be placed into smaller containers before being allowed to cool and harden, making a trauma balm which can be applied directly to injuries over joints, particularly useful for jarred fingers, toes, or injuries to the ankles, knees or elbows. The balm is massaged in using the hands and fingers and can be used in conjunction with moxa and acupressure techniques. I've found this combination to be very effective in relieving pain and restoring mobility to the injured area.

The *Jow* described above is particularly useful in treating swollen or bruised areas following body conditioning and can provide temporary pain relief as well as helping to speed up the recovery process by encouraging a good supply of fresh blood to the affected area.

*Jow* is usually the first thing to apply to an injury, and is suitable for the treatment of bruises, sprains and fractures. Note: it should not be applied to areas where the skin is broken.

**Tendon Lotion:** Tendon lotion is useful for injuries which take longer to heal such as sprains and strains. Whereas the Trauma Lotion (*Jow*) should be applied in the first few days following an injury, the Tendon lotion helps with longer term effects to tendons or ligaments. Such injuries often take a long time to recover from. Tendon Lotion encourages a good supply of blood and *Qi* to the area. It is applied by massaging it directly into the affected area.

**San Huang San:** This is used as an alternative to ice and is good for reducing swelling, inflammation and bruising. It is applied directly to the injured area as a thick paste, and then wrapped in a dressing which can be made of gauze, paper towels, bandage or a large field dressing. The good thing about using this as an alternative to ice is that although ice is very effective at reducing swelling, it can also increase the risk of stagnation of blood and fluids which can slow the recovery process. *San Huang San* uses cooling herbs which work to reduce inflammation, but also disperse stagnant blood and fluids whilst encouraging a good supply of fresh nutrients.

This can be used on any sprain, strain, pulled muscles and even fractures so long as the bone has not penetrated the skin.

**Black Ghost Oil:** This is a particularly powerful lotion which is excellent for treating bruises deep inside the muscle which cannot be seen on the surface. I've found that this type of bruising is common to the thighs following heavy conditioning. The bruising occurs to the thick muscles just above the bone rather than the surface tissue, hence the lack of visible bruising. Black Ghost Oil penetrates the tissue deeply, carrying the herbs straight to the injury rather than dispersing them over the surface tissue. This is really easy to obtain and can be used to treat many different bone bruises where the skin is not broken.

The oil is massaged directly into the affected area, and can be applied immediately following an injury for pain relief and both before and after a training session during the recovery period. This is a very powerful lotion which should only be applied whilst the bruising is still present. To provide further treatment for painful muscles once the bruising has dispersed, Black Ghost Oil should be substituted for U-I Oil.

**U-I Oil:** This massage oil helps muscles and joints which ache in cold or damp conditions, and is great for aiding lingering injuries and 'warming up' troublesome areas. It is extremely versatile in its use and can be applied immediately before training to help warm up sore or stiff parts of the body, and following training to soothe aches and pains. The ingredients used are very aromatic and also help to open the airways to make breathing easy. I have suffered a number of times with neck strains as a result of training and found U-I Oil to be excellent for treating this. It is also very good for loosening up the hamstrings and lower back prior to training, areas which are often quite tight for me, especially in cold/damp conditions.

**Yunnan Paiyao:** This powder is used for stopping bleeding and removing blood clots and can be taken internally as a capsule or applied externally directly to a cut. I will discuss here the external application. With an open wound, the powder should be applied directly before applying a dressing, direct pressure and elevation if required. The powder can also be mixed into a paste which is then spread over the wound and dressed to keep it in place. I've found this method particularly useful for treating cuts to the knuckles following *machiwara* training. For injuries such as cuts to the head where it is difficult to stop the bleeding, *Yunnan Paiyao* is particularly useful when applied directly into the wound to help stem the flow of blood. In the old days the herbs would be mixed with egg whites to make a paste. Note: *Yunnan Paiyao* **must not** be used by pregnant women.

**Moxa:** Traditionally made from mugwort, *moxa* poles are cheap, easy to obtain, and have a variety of uses. They can be used in combination with many of the oils described above, and are particularly good when paired with U-I Oil. The pole should be lit and then held at a comfortable distance away from the skin so as not to burn. The *moxa* should be moved in small circles around the injury to provide a gentle heat which spreads into the muscles, tendons and ligaments. The heat from the *moxa* helps to activate the herbs and oils present in the lotions above, whilst promoting circulation and soothing aches. I've used a combination of Trauma Balm, *Moxa* and Acupressure to treat tennis elbow type symptoms following an injury. In the later stages of recovery I used a combination of U-I Oil, *Moxa* and Acupressure. These were effective and I was able to return to full training within a matter of days.

The information presented above does not even scratch the surface when it comes to TCM, but I hope that it might capture the reader's interest in such a way that they might want to find out a little more about the healing arts.

**Habu Sake is believed to give strength to those brave enough to drink it**

# Advanced Punching Ideas

There is a great quote from Mr Tomoyose Kiei in Morio Higaonna *sensei's* *'History of Karate'* which I find really interesting. He says;

*'There are many things that Chojun sensei said that I still do not understand. For example he would say "When delivering a punch, if the recoil is lacking strength, it is no good. A straight punch is not just delivered as a straight punch. It is the same as in brush writing – a straight line is not simply drawn as a straight line."*

When I re-read this book a short time ago, this quote really jumped from the page, as it appeared to be supporting an idea I had been experimenting with in my own training. For some years I have been striking the *machiwara* with the intention not on bending the post backward, but of hitting downward toward the base. This idea was inspired by a comment from Taira Masaji *sensei* who said to me that when he punches, he tries to hit the opponent in their feet. This meant that he was sending the force downward into the opponent to collapse them forward rather than striking with an intention of knocking them backward. The opponent feels the pressure of the strike bearing down into their feet. This prevents any displacement of force, ensuring that the power of the strike stays in the target, and also, this method keeps the *ma'ai* close so that the opponent doesn't escape to create distance.

There is a famous story concerning an incident where Itosu Anko *sensei* was attacked by a group of thugs which was told by Funakoshi Gichin *sensei* in his excellent autobiography *'Karatedo My Way of Life'*. He says;

*'An eyewitness, seeing that Itosu was in no danger, rushed off to tell Azato Anko about the incident. Interrupting his account, Azato said, "And the ruffians, of course, were all lying unconscious, with their faces to the ground, were they not?" Much surprised, the witness admitted that was true, but he wondered how Azato could have known. "Very simple," replied the master. "No karate adept would be so cowardly as to attack from the rear. And should someone unfamiliar with karate attack from the front, he would end up flat on his back. But I know Itosu; his punches would knock his assailants down on their faces. I would be quite astonished if any of them survive."*[17]

This story reminded me of Taira *san's* advice on punching. The same theory also applies to *mae geri* I think, which shouldn't be performed with the aim of pushing the opponent back and distancing them, but rather,

---

[17] Karatedo My Way of Life, Funakoshi, p18

crumpling them forward and bringing them closer. This is why *mae geri* is almost always followed by *hiji'ate* in *Goju Ryu*.

Miyagi *sensei's* comparison between the drawing of a line in calligraphy and the delivery of a punch describes perfectly how to apply the strike in a manner which folds the opponent forward. The punch is delivered no differently up until the point where the strike connects with the target, but at this moment there should be a  slight dip forward with the wrist which causes the *seiken* to gouge downward into the target. The dip of the wrist should be almost invisible to the eye and is not something which changes the cosmetic appearance of the technique. It is a feeling; an intention.

The *hojo undo* tools can also be incorporated to build upon this idea. In the basic exercise using the *chiishi* where the weight is swung overhead and brought to a stop with the arm held out straight in front of the body, focus upon turning the wrist slightly inward at the focus point, ensuring that the position of the extended arm corresponds with the punching target as defined in *Sanchin*, i.e. at solar plexus height and in line with the nipple.

Another exercise which relates to this idea utilizes the *ishi sashi*. In this case the *sashi* are swung vertically above the head, and then brought slowly down to just below shoulder height. Again, there should be a pause at this point and you should focus upon dipping the wrist slightly, putting your intention downward into the target.

This method of punching is particularly useful in techniques such as *morote zuki* as found in *Gekisai Dai Ichi* and *Suparinpei*. With both hands striking simultaneously, the action of the wrist is similar to a crab claw. The top wrist gouges downward, and the bottom fist upward. There should be an intention of pinching the target between the two fists. This same idea is also applied in the double *chukoken* found in *Seipai* where the middle knuckles are extended to strike vulnerable targets on a downed opponent. Using the reduced striking surface of *chukoken* in the cursive striking manner described above is particularly painful, especially when applied into targets on the ribcage or to strike the sternum. The rolling manner in which the impact is displaced on the striking tool of *chukoken* is also less painful, meaning you can put more power into the strike with less fear of injury.

It would appear that there is a lot of wisdom hidden within Miyagi *sensei's* advice to Mr Tomoyose. It is important to go through the words of *karatedo's* pioneers with a fine tooth comb and really investigate how they can improve our understanding of even the most basic techniques of our art.

# Teaching and Perception

There reaches a point along the way where it becomes important to give back to the art that you have taken from for so many years; although this does not necessarily mean that you have to become a teacher and rush out to open your own *dojo*. The natural order of things dictates that eventually the beginner will gain experience, and through this, will develop a degree of seniority over newer students. The mistake is to think of this as a military-like rank structure. In actual fact, it has a lot more in common with how a healthy family operates. The *dojo sensei* can be thought of as the parent, the *dojo sempai* are the older brothers or sisters, and the *kohai* are the younger siblings. The parent has already gone through the growing up process and has now established themselves in the world. They will have developed an understanding of how things are done and will have formed their own opinions about what is correct and incorrect. They will, of course, have been guided and influenced by their own parents and older siblings. The *sempai*, like a good older brother, can provide advice about how to overcome problems which they themselves will have faced in the past. This experience can be of great assistance to their younger siblings who may feel too embarrassed to speak to their parents about a particular problem. The *sempai* is also expected to behave in a manner which provides a good example for their younger brothers and sisters to follow.

It is through assuming the role of the *sempai* that some really important lessons about *budo* can be learnt. By taking their first nervous steps into the realms of teaching, the practitioner will be forced to think more deeply about their own techniques so that they can demonstrate clearly something which by now, they probably perform without even thinking. This can be considered a return to the beginning, but with older eyes. In order to help and teach their *kohai* well, the *sempai* will be forced to once again assume the mindset of the beginner; to experience *shoshin*. They will have to demonstrate, pull techniques apart, analyze and critique, explain, answer questions, and bear the pressure of having their actions placed under the spotlight. Their *karate* is no longer selfish and only about themselves; it also has to include space for other people. Many people shy away from this, but I think it is an important responsibility. On top of this, the *sempai* is expected to also continue with their training and development under the watchful eyes of their own *sempai* and *sensei*.

Miyazato Eiichi *sensei* chose the name *Jundokan* for his *dojo*, based on the name of Kano Jigoro *sensei's* first *dojo*. I think this is a great name, with a very deep meaning. The *kanji* for *Jun* means 'submit; order; series'. When combined with the *kanji* for *Do*, the term represents 'following the natural order of the way'. This term is commonly simplified to meaning 'next in line'. The manner of teaching at the *Jundokan* under Miyazato *sensei* followed this ideal by having no set classes. Under these circumstances students were taught not to rely upon being spoon-fed information, and so had to take responsibility for themselves. If a student was lazy, they were neglected, but if a student showed enthusiasm and worked hard, they were given help and encouragement. *Sempai* looked after *kohai* both inside and outside the *dojo*, and this created a healthy atmosphere which was beneficial to everyone. Students of all ages would share the *dojo* floor and the *sempai* would take time out from their own training to help their *kohai* progress. This is the natural order of the way. Babies become children, children become adults, adults become parents, and so the cycle flourishes and continues.

Instructing is easy, but teaching is extremely difficult. This is the difference between an instructor and a *sensei*. Unlike other areas of *karate*, you do not get taught how to teach. This is something which you must learn for yourself as you go along, taking examples from the people who have helped you in your own development. It is important to recognize the problems of a student and be able to identify similar struggles which you have faced yourself, and remember what you did in order to overcome them. How did your own *sensei* assist you with this, and were there any particular lessons which forced you to 'wake up' and catch hold of an idea or feeling. Also, what did you do wrong during your own battles and how can you assist your *kohai* with avoiding similar pitfalls. Sometimes though, it is best to allow the *kohai* to make mistakes in order to learn from them. This is a very difficult thing to do and is not something to be taken lightly. It can be very tough standing by, watching while a person who you care about struggles, but occasionally this is exactly what you must do. Teaching is a serious responsibility!

Over time, the physical gives way to matters concerning the spirit. This provides an even greater challenge, but also richer rewards. An understanding of human nature, psychology, motivation, leadership, problem solving, camaraderie, physiology, relationships and a whole host of other areas is required in order to effectively teach *karatedo* as both *budo* and *bujutsu*. It requires you to get inside the mind of another person in order to foresee the present, and the future. There is nothing mystical about this; it simply requires that the teacher has experienced for themselves what they are asking the student to do. An example of this is austere training (*shugyo*), where the student will be pushed to the limits of their physical capabilities in order to develop the spirit. If the teacher has not undergone such hardship themselves, it is impossible for them to understand what the student is feeling, and how best to help them when their spirit begins to falter. This is shameful. The term *sensei* means 'a person who has lived before' which implies that they have already experienced what the student is facing. This is essential if they are to be of any use to the student.

Every student is different, each with their own unique strengths, weaknesses, and character traits. The method of teaching has to be adapted to best approach each set of individual circumstances. There is no 'one size fits all' method. This is why *karate* teachers typically only had a handful of students. Any more than this would cause too many headaches for the teacher who has to bear the problems of those following him, as well as their own! The difference between a *sensei* and an excellent *sensei* is that the latter is able to perceive what is going on inside the head of the student. He does this by carefully observing the characteristics of the individual student by setting them various tasks and evaluating their performance. Over time, people reveal their true nature, and training in *karatedo* reveals this nature very quickly indeed. Once an idea about the personality of a student has been formulated, the *sensei* can then plan a strategy which best suits their future martial education. Make no mistake, an excellent *sensei* can read you like a book. I'm sure you will have met a teacher like this at some point and will understand what I mean. This overall strategy is continually refined over time as the student loses certain characteristics and develops new ones, presenting an ever changing problem for the *sensei* to help solve.

The insights into human nature which are gained through such teaching experiences enable human development. This transcends being merely a martial artist. In Okinawa, certain *karate sensei* were respected leaders of their local communities. This had nothing to do with their physical skills, but rather, their wisdom. If you were unsure whether your latest business idea was likely to be successful, you would go consult with Kinjo *Tanmei*, 'he always knows what to do'. I need a new roof put on the house but I'm not sure of a builder I can trust. I know, I'll ask Higa *sensei*, 'he always has good advice'. This was, and still is, the kind of respect which is afforded to good *sensei* in Okinawa. Many times I have been with particular *sensei* when a stranger has come to the *dojo* to ask advice about something completely unrelated to *karate*.

*Karate* develops insight and perception. It enables you to read other people and see their true intentions. These skills are learnt by teaching others. The usefulness of such skills in relation to self-defense and life in general should be obvious to all. This of course, is only the case where *karate* is taught in the correct manner. The individualistic, personal training methods which you read about in the history books produced so many great masters because this is the correct way to teach *karate*. When these methods are substituted for membership, money, fame or position; you will learn little about yourself, or your fellow beings. You might get a nice car out of it though......

**Hokama *sensei* teaching the finer points of *kata* application**

# Stealing The Initiative

One of the most common techniques found within the *kata* of *Goju Ryu* is the *Chudan Uke*, and its many variants such as *mawashi uke, kake uke, ura uke, koken uke, sukui uke*, etc. Every single *kata* contains this posture, and most commonly it is performed following a turn. There are some interesting points which are raised from this, and some good principles which can be applied depending upon the type of situation or opponent.

*Goju Ryu* is at its most effective when a point of contact is established with the opponent. This is why so much time is spent practicing *kakie*, so that you learn to read the intentions of an opponent through the point of contact which is established at the meeting of the arms between attacker and defender. Once this position is established, it becomes much easier to defend against the random strikes of your opponent, rather than standing at *kumite* range and relying on eyesight alone to pick up on the opponent's intentions. Action is always faster than reaction, so this method makes it very difficult to prevent yourself from being hit. Establishing a point of contact allows the body to 'feel' what is happening in order to assist the eyes, developing a much earlier cue to act upon. Experiment with a partner in order to experience this by having them stand within striking range to deliver attacks completely at random which you must then attempt to defend. The level of power used should be adjusted accordingly or protective equipment used. Without covering up like in boxing, blocking the attacks will prove quite difficult. Next, perform the same exercise but from either single or double hand *kakie* position. You will find that you are able to successfully defend a much higher percentage of your partner's strikes. Playing with this exercise for 5 minutes or so should give you a good idea about the importance of establishing a point of contact with the opponent.

When we turn in *kata*, using a variant of *Chudan Uke* to exit the turning motion, it is exactly this point of contact that we're trying to establish. The covering arm provides protection to the face as we turn toward an unknown threat, and following this, the opposite hand then reaches forward to engage with the opponent's limbs. From this contact point, our response is then initiated. This idea can be likened to an Octopus stretching out its tentacles in order to feel for its prey. The 'blocking' hand should have the intention of reaching, searching, and clearing, linking, sticking and dominating. The mindset of such 'blocking' techniques should not be defensive; they require a strong, determined, assertive attitude.

For example, when turning 180 degrees to the rear, imagine that a person has pushed you from behind. As you step offline and turn to face the threat, the hands are up, covering the face whilst you turn the body. From this position, the hands reach forward to engage and connect. Once the contact is made, the *Sanchin* structure enables you to dominate and overpower in order to break the opponent's posture and develop an opening. There are occasions in *kata* too where the threat is right on top of us, making this tactic unviable. On these occasions, *teisho* is used to distance the opponent and buy time, such as in *Seisan* and *Suparinpei*.

The contact point must also be 'live'. By this I mean that it has to remain dominant. It is no good if once contact is made; the arm is then overpowered by the opponent so that they regain the initiative. This arm should be considered the protective barrier; a shield to hide behind whilst you deliver your attack, like with the *tinbe* and *rochin*. It can be likened to walking through a fast revolving door. The contact arm reaches out to stop or slow the movement of the door so that you can safely enter without being hit. The counter strikes are allowed to operate due to the support provided by the contact arm. This should be considered carefully in *Sanchin kata*. Many people place their intention in the punching arm and neglect the blocking arm, allowing it to move or otherwise lose strength. This is a mistake. As the punch is delivered, particular care should be taken to ensure the blocking arm maintains dominance. If anything, more attention should be paid to the blocking arm than the punching arm.

Upon achieving a contact with the opponent, it is important that the blocking arm then seizes the initiative immediately. This is achieved not only through unbalancing and breaking their posture, but more effectively through the use of 'threat'. What I mean by 'threat' is stealing the centerline and aiming a striking tool on target, ready to be immediately deployed if the opponent moves. This idea is best appreciated in the practice of *Kobudo* I have found, because having a *Sai* pointing directly at your eye really makes you take notice of the importance of having a weapon ready on target. The same is true of *Uke Waza*. After creating a point of contact and clearing the opponent's limbs from your own centerline, your fist or hand should then establish a position so that the striking tool is pointing directly at your opponents face or throat. The intention should also be of pressing forward, rather than simply maintaining position. You must put the opponent on the back foot with this movement, taking away their will to move forward. This is stealing the initiative. For example, *kake uke* is often taught to be performed with the intention of blocking a strike to then grab and pull the opponent off balance. My idea is a little different because I believe that pulling backward takes away from the momentum of pressing forward, which is what we should be looking to achieve. It is also extremely difficult to grab a fast moving limb, especially with any real strength. Once the *kake uke* has completed its initial task of defending the opponents strike, I believe that establishing dominance of the centerline becomes more important than seizing the limb. After blocking, have the intention of putting the open palm directly into the opponents face. This not only unbalances and stops their momentum, but is also makes it difficult for them to see in order to accurately target you with further strikes. In the meantime you are also delivering your own counter strikes under the security provided by the contact limb.

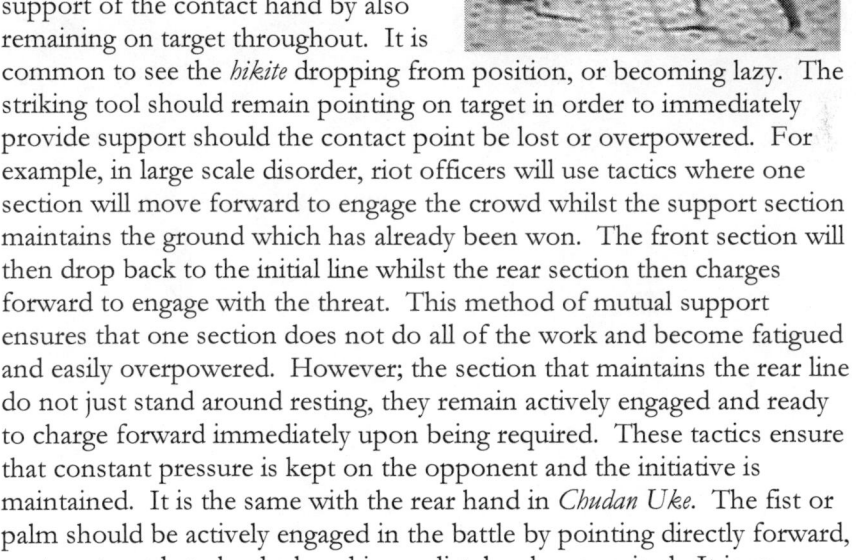

This is difficult to explain properly with words, but the important point to consider is threatening the opponents face through your use of posture in order to halt their momentum. This is the job of the *Sanchin* structure, and the link between *Sanchin*, *Kata*, *Kakie* and *Jissen*.

The rear hand too must act in support of the contact hand by also remaining on target throughout. It is common to see the *hikite* dropping from position, or becoming lazy. The striking tool should remain pointing on target in order to immediately provide support should the contact point be lost or overpowered. For example, in large scale disorder, riot officers will use tactics where one section will move forward to engage the crowd whilst the support section maintains the ground which has already been won. The front section will then drop back to the initial line whilst the rear section then charges forward to engage with the threat. This method of mutual support ensures that one section does not do all of the work and become fatigued and easily overpowered. However; the section that maintains the rear line do not just stand around resting, they remain actively engaged and ready to charge forward immediately upon being required. These tactics ensure that constant pressure is kept on the opponent and the initiative is maintained. It is the same with the rear hand in *Chudan Uke*. The fist or palm should be actively engaged in the battle by pointing directly forward, on target, ready to be deployed immediately when required. It is an important shift in mindset from defensive to offensive.

If, while the rear hand is travelling forward to strike, the contact limb detects a change in pressure to indicate that the opponent is about to move or attack; the contact hand can immediately strike forward into the face to maintain the initiative. This is the importance of stealing the centerline and maintaining dominance through posture.

The *chudan uke kamae* is one of the most basic elements of *Goju Ryu* but it is important to study it deeply and investigate various ways of how it can be used to change the rhythm of a fight.

**Chudan Uke Kamae is the primary position of Goju Ryu**

# Go & Ju Of Conflict Management

I enjoy watching and studying people. I think that practicing *karatedo* over an extended period of time encourages this in order to highlight any shortcomings in our own characters, and also to look for positive traits in other people which we can emulate in order to better ourselves. Having been involved professionally in conflict management for many years, the skills I have developed to a small degree at reading other people have been of great benefit and have helped me to avoid physical conflict with a fairly high rate of success. In fact, I am quietly proud of how many fights I have managed to talk my way out of. No easy feat considering I deal almost exclusively with the kind of people who would think little of cheating, hurting, or killing another person if the need arose. Despite this, there are occasions where no amount of communication, psychology, posturing, or avoidance will help; and at such times there is no alternative but to act decisively and take control of the other person both physically and mentally, but I firmly believe that such occasions are a rarity and most conflicts can be solved without resorting to violence.

By applying the principles of hard/soft to our interactions with other people, we can usually avoid conflict. It is very strange how we human beings seem to be able to connect and communicate without a single word being said. Consider how when one person yawns, it often causes us to do the same, or how laughter is so infectious. Our moods are also affected by the people around us, and this has quite serious implications for both self-defense and how we live our lives. A person who is always complaining loudly about their situations and is miserable often causes the people around them to become depressed. In families or teams this can lead to defeat from within. On the contrary, if such an individual is surrounded by positive and lively people, this will have a good effect upon them and help improve their outlook on life. The impact that our immediate friendship groups have upon our mental wellbeing cannot be overemphasized, so we should be very careful about the company we keep.

In Okinawa the sun is usually shining and there are blue skies, lush green hills, azure seas, and brightly coloured flowers outside of the main cities. Because of this people are very happy, friendly, courteous, and generally live long, contented lives. The pace of life is slower, and folks are naturally quite laid back. Compare this to the various cities around the world where the buildings are so high that they obscure the sky, the air is polluted and everything appears grey, it is too crowded, and everybody is rushing around all of the time, competing and trying to get ahead of the next man. This leads to conflict and everybody becoming stressed. This is why there are so many aggressive people around these days. Human beings, like plants, need sun. If a person is cooped up all day and surrounded by grey, this is no good for their general wellbeing and can lead to increased levels of stress. With so many people experiencing varying levels of stress in their daily lives, it is little wonder that there is so much conflict in the world. You can see this from the way people board trains, queue in traffic, walk the streets and communicate with one another. It came as no surprise to me that so many chose to get involved in the rioting which happened in London during the summer of 2011. Youngsters in the UK from certain parts of the country hold zero regard for other people or for the consequences of their actions. This, I am quite sure, is due to them growing up surrounded by so much negativity from their environment, family groups, friendship networks, and the media which encourages people to think it's cool to be a bad guy.

Developing an understanding of yourself and your personality through *karate* training is important and leads to an understanding of human nature in general. It is essential that you learn to read the mind of an opponent in order to understand what they hope to achieve through their particular conflict. In order to do this, you must be able to remove yourself emotionally from the encounter. The moment you begin to take insults personally or rise to an opponent's aggression levels, you begin to lose control of the situation, and the options available to escape without violence quickly begin to diminish. Detachment allows you to see things clearly and decide upon tactics and strategies to defeat the opponent. If the other person is angry at you for a driving mistake and is shouting and swearing at you, it would be best to simply apologize for driving like an idiot and not paying attention, even if you were not at fault. If an aggressor is intimating to you that he has a knife and wants your wallet, it is far better to hand the wallet over rather than die in a ditch to keep hold of your credit cards which could be cancelled anyway. If a guy is sleazing over your wife at the bar, take it as a compliment and treat her to drinks at a different, quieter bar. Most of the time the other person simply wants a positive outcome for themselves, be it an ego boost, some easy money which they didn't earn themselves, or simply the fact that 'they were right' about something quite pointless. None of these reasons are something to worry yourself about or become pushed into a situation where you might lose your life or get arrested, for these are two very possible outcomes for those who willingly choosing to take part in a fight.

I should specify here that a fight is very different to self-defense. A fight is something which you make a conscious decision to become a part of, whereas self-defense is forced upon you and there is no other alternative but to use force in order to escape (hopefully) safely. The difference should be considered carefully.

Responding to a *Go* situation with *Go* uses force against force, and the stronger force will always win. By responding with *Ju* it is possible to absorb *Go* and nullify its effects. This can lead to 'victory without contention' or as Miyagi *sensei* put it 'peace without incident'. In personal life, if your wife is angry, it is best to say sorry and be soft. Responding angrily will only make the situation worse and create an unbearable atmosphere. It is very hard to remain angry at somebody who refuses to argue back. Miyagi *sensei* would always apologize to a person rather than become drawn into a fight.

Responding to an opponent who is calculated, calm, and intelligent is much more difficult than dealing with people who are angry and aggressive. The latter can be easily tricked, for they rarely notice the subtleties of tactics and psychology. This makes it very easy to divert their attention one way and then attack from another. I am not necessarily referring to physical techniques here! Seizing the opponents mind is very important with regards to taking the initiative in an encounter. A *Ju* opponent makes this much more difficult as they will not provide you with so many clues. It can be quite unnerving facing somebody who does not appear fazed by anything. Whereas a *Go* opponent can dominate and shock their victim into defeat, a *Ju* opponent does this through implied danger which can quickly defeat their victim mentally. I have had opponents say to me before an encounter 'I know where your family live'. Although I knew this to be an empty threat, the ploy had the desired effect of taking the initiative early in the encounter because for a moment, my mind was worrying about other things rather than the opponent in front of me. Another example of this happened to a friend of mine during an MMA bout. He hit his opponent with a solid right, sending him to the mat with his first punch, but the opponent rolled backwards with the momentum and sprang to his feet, saying 'yeah, I like being hit like that!' My friend was shocked, and the opponent went on to defeat him later in the bout. A *Ju* opponent is much more difficult I think.

Switching between the two extremes of *Go* and *Ju* with regards to the mindset you display to the opponent during an encounter can be an effective tool. Leading an opponent to believe you are weak where really you are strong is a tactic which has been used for centuries, and is one of the principal areas covered in Sun Tzu's Art of War. This however, is something which is very difficult for the majority of us. The ego is a very hard thing to control, and we rarely want be appear weak in front of other people. It is much more natural for people to act strong when really they are weak. This is also a useful tactic on certain occasions, but if it is discovered to be false it can be exploited easily by a strong opponent. Miyagi Chojun *sensei* referred to this as *fuuna*. Madambashi Keiyo stated;

*When I arrived at Chojun sensei's house I said to him, "Please teach me te." Chojun sensei replied, "There are many forms of te: there is sodi (true martial arts), uduidi (dancing martial arts), inakadi (country – superficial – martial arts) and asobidi (playful – for enjoyment- martial arts). Which one do you wish to learn?"*

*I replied, "I wish to learn sodi."*

*Sensei then told me, "Do not act with fuuna." "What is fuuna?" I asked. He replied, "Chuba fuuna is to act as if you are strong even though you are weak, and nai fuuna is acting as if you can do something when in fact you cannot. You must not act in this way," he told me sternly.* [18]

It is important to recognize when an opponent is demonstrating *fuuna* and quickly take advantage of it. On such occasions responding with *Go* is the best option in order to immediately destroy their spirit. Again, this can be achieved without resorting to physical means.

I must stress the importance of knowing what the opponent wants to achieve. A mugger wants your money, a person with a giant ego wants to have that ego stoked in front of others, and an idiot wants to remain blind to the fact that they are indeed, an idiot. All of these people can be dealt with without fighting. The dangerous psychopath who just wants to attack somebody is actually a rarity, and on such occasions there is no option but to respond with force and make your escape. In all of these situations, *karate* has many uses.

---

[18] The History of Karate, Higaonna, p176

# Animal Methods In Goju Ryu

*'The most ancient methods of Chinese kempo were first based on the fighting movements of birds and beasts. Hence, the names of the individual methods of fighting that reflected the source from which they ascended. By mere example: the tiger way, the lion way, the monkey way, the dog way, and the way of the crane.'* Miyagi Chojun[19]

The kata of *Goju Ryu* consist of a multitude of *kamae*, each describing ways of both offense and defense. The outer appearance of such *kamae* provides us with only the shell; a brief snapshot from which it can be difficult to discern the 'before and after' of an individual technique. In order to use the various techniques to their fullest potential the correct intent and psychological aspects need to be added to the movements. In addition to this, the correct set up of such techniques is further enhanced through a study of the animal methods of body movement.

That animal inspired techniques are contained within the *kata* of *Goju Ryu* should come as no great surprise considering the early influence of Kojo Taitei upon Higashionna Kanryo *sensei*, and the significant impact that the Chinese martial arts had upon the development of *Nahadi* in general from the various teachers of the Matsuyama group. But *Kojo Ryu* contains no single *kata* which are the same as *Goju Ryu*, not even *Sanchin*.[20] If this is the case, what did Higashionna *sensei* actually learn from Kojo Taitei during the early days of his training? According to Patrick McCarthy, applications were historically taught before *kata*, with the *kata* remaining a closely guarded secret only to be passed onto the inner students, or in the case of *Kojo Ryu*, family members. I asked Hokama *sensei* about whether elements of *Kojo Ryu* can still be found in *Goju Ryu* and he said that the teachings can only be found in the applications.[21] With the *Kojo Ryu kata* focusing so much upon the movements of animals, it is my opinion that the legacy of the Kojo teachings which Higashionna *sensei* received may actually be found in the animal methods of body movement. (Note – I learnt these methods from Hokama Tetsuhiro *sensei* at his *dojo* in Nishihara. Hokama *sensei* received teaching from many different sources outside of *Goju Ryu* and many of his skills are considered quite rare these days. It is said that as well as being a student of Higa Seko *sensei* and Fukuchi Seiko *sensei*, he also received instruction from Nakasone Seiryu who had studied directly under Miyagi *sensei* for a short period. Nakasone

---

[19] Ancient Okinawan Martial Arts, Volume Two, McCarthy, p45

[20] conversation with Joe Swift, London 2011

[21] conversation with Hokama sensei, Nishihara, 2011

*sensei* was primarily a practitioner of *Tomaridi* and had a large influence upon the *Gohakukai* stream of *Goju Ryu*. In the days of the *Matsuyama* study group there were frequent exchanges of ideas between the masters of *Nahadi* and *Tomaridi* and it is quite possible that certain parts of practice which failed to be handed down through one stream might still be preserved in another. This provides an exciting avenue for further research)

I cannot recommend highly enough the article written by Mr Joe Swift and Mr Mario McKenna 'A Brief Overview of the Etymology of Modern Goju Ryu Karate-Do Kata'. This comprehensive essay makes for fascinating reading and provides useful background information regarding the inclusion of animal inspired techniques within the *kata* of *Goju Ryu*, as well as alternate renderings of the *kata kanji* which support their theories.

In order to provide an insight into the use and appearance of each animal, a brief explanation of the characteristics and application of some of the more common methods will be given.

### Crane

The crane is one of the principal methods contained within the *Goju Ryu* system which borrows heavily from the Southern Chinese White Crane traditions. Associated with swiftness and flexibility, the crane method is believed to strengthen the body's sinews. Making frequent use of the elbows and wrists to defend, and the fingertips, back of the hands and the wrists to attack, the crane is a soft/hard method which is perfectly suited to the principles of *Goju Ryu*. This method also makes use of the straight leg and toe tips to kick against targets on the lower body, making them very difficult to defend.

## Tiger

The tiger is the partner in the relationship between the tiger and crane. These can be considered brother and sister, *Go* and *Ju*. The tiger is characterized by aggressive hard, fast movements, which are believed to strengthen the bones and is one of the more familiar animal styles within *Goju Ryu*. Kata such as *sanseiru*, *seisan* and

*suparinpei* make frequent use of tiger type techniques such as seizing the throat, double palm strikes, *ippon ken*, twisting the head to break the neck, and clawing into vulnerable areas such as the void behind the collar bone.

## Hawk

The hawk is very important with regard to forming a protective barrier around the body in order to shrug off an assailant and throw them to the ground. This idea is contained within the double *nukite* sequence of

*Sanchin kata*. The key with this technique is to make the upper back strong, like a protective shell.

The hawk method also makes use of the fingertips to seize and inflict pain upon an opponent. The claws are trained using the *nigiri gami*, whereas the beak is imitated by pinching vulnerable targets on the opponent using the thumb and forefinger as performed during *Kin'na waza* following entangling and restraining. The idea implied here is that when hunting for

food, the hawk first uses its claws to catch its prey and immobilize, and then once secured it uses its beak to finish. *Seiunchin kata* best exemplifies this method.

## Snake

The snake is believed to cultivate a person's essence and is characterized by coiling power, flexibility and entangling limbs (*karamadi*). After immobilizing its prey the snake finishes by choking or biting, using its

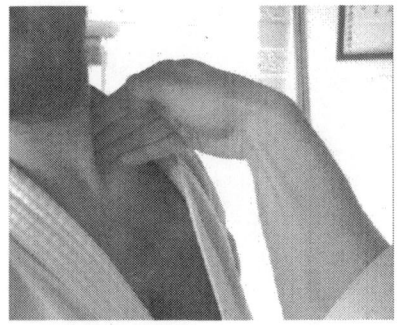

fangs to inject venom. The fingertips can also used to distract and 'hypnotize' an opponent, which means to steal their attention and create an opening. The snake way uses the tendons of the wrist to flex and engage in order to break free from wrist grabs and makes the fingers strong like the fangs of a *Habu* in order to gouge and pierce vulnerable targets.

Monkey

Characterized by playfulness and instinctive movement, the monkey uses 'dead weight' strikes such as *tettsui uchi* to hit through a target. This method enables the practitioner to make their body heavy whilst delivering powerful strikes using the palms, elbows and forearms from very close range. The monkey style also emphasizes the use of the shoulders in order to create space to escape from front and rear bear hugs. Shaking and wriggling are characteristics of the monkey method, moving the shoulders in an up/down circular fashion to make it difficult for an opponent to maintain their hold. This particular method used to be practiced

against tree trunks, using the forearms, elbows, shoulders, chest, and hips to strike from close range whilst keeping a constant point of contact like in *kakie*. Modern MMA practitioners make frequent use of a monkey technique whilst fighting on the ground when they trap the opponent between their legs in 'the guard'.

Dog

Dog methods are exemplified by attacks to the legs of the opponent either from a standing position or more commonly, from the ground. These techniques provide useful defenses for occasions where you may find yourself on your back against a standing opponent. The feet are used to entangle  and upset the balance of the enemy whilst at the same time, providing mobility on the ground so that you do not become a static target. The legs are also used to kick up at the opponent to keep them at a safe distance. It is interesting to see that the dog methods are commonly used in Mixed Martial Arts and they still create problems for the standing fighter who is often unable to pass through the legs to press their attack.

Fish

This method imitates the powerful yet flowing movements of a fish's tail as it moves through the water. Characterized as a *Ju* method of both blocking and striking, fish techniques generate a type of power which is able to penetrate deep into the target, bypassing the protective muscle barrier of the abdomen in order to strike the internal organs directly. Against organs which contain a lot of fluid, this method of attack is particularly dangerous. *Tensho kata* makes frequent use of this way.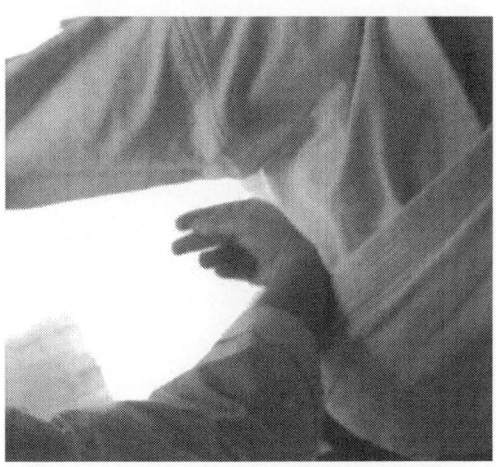

Suiken (Drunken Fist)

Although not classified as an animal method per se, the drunken fist is a unique way of using the body which is common to many styles of Okinawan *karate* and is also discussed in the *Bubishi*. The drunken fist utilizes unpredictability and the skill to rebound from an opponent's attack in order to deliver a surprise rapid counter. This method makes use

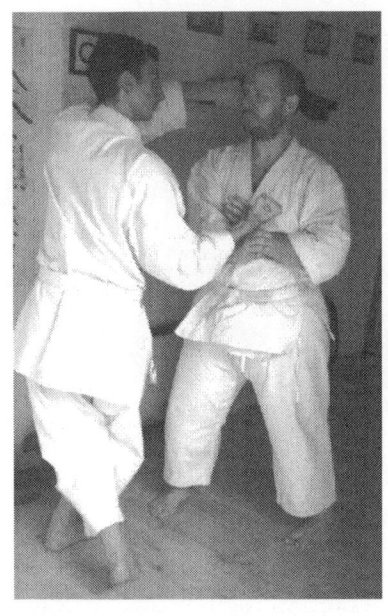
of *Ju* style strikes to hit using a dead weight whilst sinking and spiraling the body to generate powerful centrifugal force. The drunken fist also teaches tactical methods of hiding your attack and misleading an opponent in order to expose a target. As it is written in the *Bubishi* 'if you want to attack the East, first move West'. *Seipai* and *saifa kata* make frequent use of the *suiken* method.

The various animal methods described here are presented individually as stand-alone techniques to serve as a brief introduction to this study. In actual use, the ways combine and blend together seamlessly in order to enhance the application of *kata* sequences. In addition to the various methods presented in this article, there are many more which are also contained within the *kata* of *Goju Ryu* including mantis, dragon, turtle, caterpillar, seahorse, elephant, horse and bear. Some of these techniques relate to martial application, whereas others are more associated with health and *Kiko* (Qigong).

Like all animals, human beings are born with a natural instinct to protect themselves. The most obvious example of this is the stress response known as fight or flight. Such responses make a number of physiological changes within the body and stem from how our ancestors responded to threats against their lives. This is our primal animalistic nature. Hokama *sensei* told me;

"Outside the *dojo* we are people, and courtesy is very important, but inside the *dojo* we have to become like animals and use every weapon on our body."

Children seem to have the greatest link to this in the way they naturally behave and play. As we get older we lose this connection with nature and start to act in ways which are considered more socially acceptable and our natural instincts become dulled. From my experience, the most difficult opponents to face are women, persons suffering from mental illness, and people who are under the influence of drugs. This is because they do not behave like regular opponents. Women will bite, spit, scratch, pull hair, scrape their feet into your shins and scream in your face. These are useful self-defense techniques which we were all born with, but which men in particular lose as they become indoctrinated into fighting according to

Queensbury rules. Most boys are told from an early age to play fair and abide by the rules, but in self-defense there is no such thing as a fair fight. This is something which many 'decent' people have difficulty coming to terms with. Practicing in accordance with the animal methods highlights some of the natural responses which lie dormant within all of us, waiting to be rediscovered. They are a reminder of the various tricks at our disposal which could create just enough space or distraction to enable us to escape a hostile attacker.

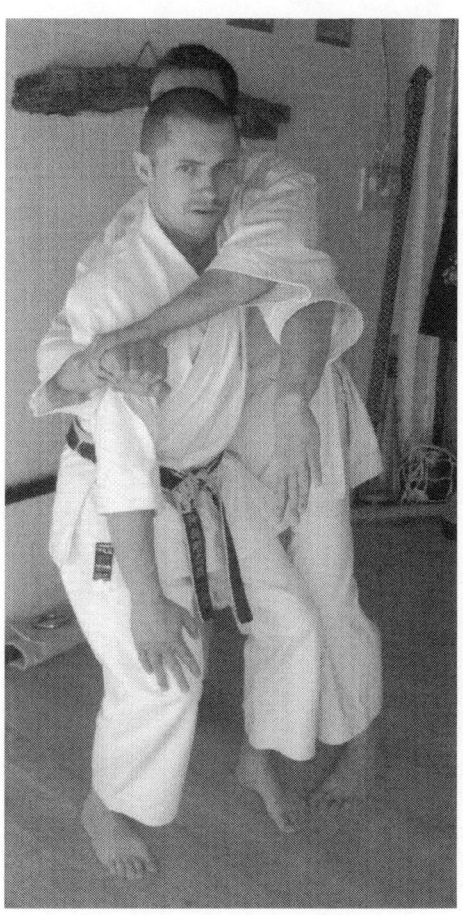

# Okinawa 2011

## Arrival

It was with many mixed feelings that I prepared to return to Okinawa and the *dojo* of Hokama Tetsuhiro *sensei* in the February of 2011. Of course I was excited and looking forward to experiencing the events which would unfold and also to see, hear, taste, and feel the birthplace of *karate* once again, but on the other hand I was well aware of how homesick I would become due to leaving my family and familiar surroundings. My son had been born only 6 months earlier and this would be the first time I had left him for more than a day. Having visited Okinawa a number of times previously alone, I was all too familiar with how lonely I often feel out there. Despite being completely in love with the island, I often can't wait

to return home to familiarity and I was sure that this would be much worse now that I had my son to think about. The personal worries I was facing were of course all part of the experience, and are quite essential to our growth as *karateka* and people. It is very easy to become overly relaxed around the familiar and to fall into the trap of being afraid to ever leave our comfort zone. I think this is a common problem which confronts many people, causing them to take the easier option rather than facing the unknown. As difficult as facing the unknown can sometimes be, I think once the unknown becomes 'known' it can actually be much harder. *Goju Ryu* requires a certain mindset from the practitioner though and such a character is only forged through challenge so it is important to make the most of such opportunities and face them with a strong spirit.

I was extremely fortunate this time to be sharing the experience with my *sensei* Richard Barrett, my *sempai* Mark Sessions, my favorite writer since childhood Mike Clarke *sensei*, and his student Mitch. Barrett sensei, Mark and I would be travelling together from London, and the plan was that we would be met at Naha airport by Clarke *sensei* and Mitch, but we were to be met by a number of unfortunate incidents before we even set foot on Okinawa.

Now, I would like to present my theory that this whole chain of events was started by Mark. First of all, his father was kindly picking me up from my house in order to take us all to the airport. Mark gave terrible directions which resulted in his father missing the turning on the motorway, meaning he had to drive a further 10 miles before he could turn around and go back at the next exit, which at 0400am would be enough to cause a sense of humor failure from anyone! Next, at the airport Mark lost his wallet containing all of his money for Okinawa and his credit cards which caused a minor panic, and threw a further spanner into the works of a so far eventful morning. Luckily the security staff found they had simply misplaced it and were able to return it to Mark. From this point on things got steadily worse as our flight times from Paris were changed which resulted in us missing our connecting flight from Tokyo to Okinawa. I would suggest that this too was in some way caused by Mark. Then upon arrival at Tokyo we were informed that our luggage had been left at London and would not be arriving in Okinawa for at least 3 days!!

With our arrival in Okinawa now some 3 hours later than expected, we discovered that Clarke *sensei* and Mitch had already been and gone, fearing that we had missed our flights or been arrested. This presented another problem as Barrett *sensei* did not have the address of the *Ryokan* where he would be staying with Clarke *sensei*. With this in mind we quickly rushed to *Heiwa Dori* to buy a spare T-shirts, underwear and some products to clean ourselves, and then quickly made our way to the *Jundokan* to track down Clarke *sensei*. We were informed by Sunagawa *san* that he would be there around 7pm so we returned a short time later where we finally met up with Clarke *sensei* and Mitch. This in itself was no mean feat for Clarke *sensei* and Mitch had travelled from Tasmania, Mark and I from London, and Barrett *sensei* from Spain. The fact that we had all managed to be in Okinawa at the same time was quite an achievement we thought! It was good to catch up for an all too short a time, but already Mark and I had to rush off to get to the *Kenshikan*. We all arranged to meet up again the following day and said our goodbyes for the evening.

Making our way to the *Kenshikan* by Monorail and Taxi, we arrived without further incident and were greeted by Hokama *sensei* at the *dojo*. Receiving a warm welcome and sitting down at that familiar old table to drink some more familiar *bubishi* tea, we explained the events of our journey so far and began to plan the rest of our stay with him. Hokama *sensei* told us that we would begin the next day by visiting Nishihara where he was teaching group *Bo Taiso* session in a local community center. This all sounded very interesting to me, and I began to wonder what *Bo Taiso* would consist of? With no further explanation we were shown up to our room to leave what little personal possessions we still had on us, and we were then taken to a local restaurant for dinner, which was much appreciated and a very kind gesture. I was still wondering what *Bo Taiso* was and asked a number of times, but Hokama *sensei* skillfully evaded the question, leaving it for us to find out the following day. Following dinner we said our goodbyes for the evening and settled down for some much needed sleep. Already it had been an eventful 24 hours and we felt many moons away from England and familiarity.

### **Training Begins**

An interesting incident had occurred the previous day which I forgot to mention. From Naha airport we took the monorail to *Makishi* station, near to *Heiwa Dori* where we would frantically rush around trying to buy spare clothes due to our luggage having gone missing. The monorail gets fairly busy in central Naha, but being first on the train at the airport, the three of us all had seats. There were a couple of middle aged ladies sat opposite gossiping loudly about various subjects, and I used this opportunity to practice my Japanese by trying to follow their conversation. A few stops further, two elderly ladies got on board the carriage and could not find a seat, so we immediately gave up ours. The gossiping ladies remarked to one another that we must be *karate* students. It was nice to see that *karate* is still thought of by some people in such terms, and I was pleased that our minor actions had shown the art in a good light.

The following morning Mark and I awoke early to practice *Sanchin* in the

*dojo*. We were joined by Hokama *sensei* a short time later who invited us upstairs to his home for breakfast. This was to be a daily occurrence and the breakfasts were enormous and quite delicious. The conversations over breakfast were varied and always interesting, covering subjects from *karate* to world history and architecture. As an archaeologist, Hokama *sensei* displays a passion for all areas related to history, and his ability to relate every subject back to *karate* is quite impressive. Most of these conversations will remain private between us so I would urge you to visit in order to learn more about his ideas.

Following our hefty breakfast we made our way to *Tomari* by Taxi and the Monorail, passing *Shurijo* along the way and affording Mark his first view of this famous site. Getting off at *Makishi* station and walking through the backstreets to *Tomari*, passing the *Sogenji* stone gate en route, we arrived on time at *Shureido* where we had arranged to meet Barrett *sensei*, Clarke *sensei* and Mitch. I was delighted to see that they were already inside and running around like excited kids in a sweet shop. We greeted everybody and it was good fun to see that Nakasone *san* had found a few old photographs from when Barrett *sensei* was there during the 80's. The staff members at *Shureido* are among the friendliest in the world, and I always have a great time whenever I visit the store. The serious stuff quickly began though, for we needed new *dogi* and belts so that we could begin training as ours were at this time 30,000 feet up in the air somewhere between London and Tokyo. A short time later we were fully equipped with fresh new training attire and ready for training!

Grabbing a quick lunch together at a traditional Okinawan restaurant, we said goodbye and all went our separate ways to begin our days training. Mark and I returned to the *Kenshikan*, and changed into our brand new *dogi* and shiny new belts, already feeling quite awkward outside of the familiarity of my tatty old training wear. Hokama *sensei* appeared with a grin and we helped him to load a stack of *Bo* into the back of his car and we then drove together to a local community center in *Nishihara* town.

Entering through the door we were met by an old lady who appeared to be in her 90's who aggressively instructed us to remove our shoes. We were then ushered into a side room where a number of chairs had been set out in a semi-circle. Already inside the room were a few more ladies, all appearing to be over 70 years old. I now felt completely awkward, standing in my shiny new *dogi* with everybody staring at me as though I were the only person to turn up at a party having been tricked into believing it was fancy dress! Suddenly it all dropped into place and I discovered what *Bo Taiso* actually was. This was to be a gentle health and exercise class for old people, not village *kumi bo* as I had mistakenly thought. The room soon filled to capacity and Hokama *sensei* delivered his welcome speech, following which we were encouraged to also give speeches as is the custom. Once formalities were over we were straight into training, using the *Bo* to augment various *junbi undo* exercises and stretches to encourage mobility and gentle muscle use, each movement combined with correct breathing. A degree of concern began to set in as I started to break a sweat and my breathing quickened along with my burning muscles. This was NOT gentle exercise for old people; this was as much a lesson for us into how keeping a flexible, healthy body can enhance our general wellbeing into our twilight years. These amazing ladies displayed a flexibility that completely put us to shame. Their bodies had the suppleness of babies, and the various postures which stressed our bodies were held quite comfortably by the rest of the group, much to our embarrassment. The necessity for balance between *Go* and *Ju* was brought to our attention in a remarkable way and I was deeply impressed by everybody present. As well as the usual *junbi undo* exercises relating to the various joints and muscles of the body, there were additional ones relating to the practice of *Qigong* and the *Ekkinkyo* where various parts of the body were massaged in order to promote the flow of *Qi* and prevent stagnation. This, it was explained by Hokama *sensei*, related deeply to the study of *Sanchin*.

Following training we all sat around a low table together for tea and sweets. It was great spending the afternoon in such a way and to experience a side of Okinawa which is rarely seen by visitors. The conversation flowed, and the lady who appeared initially skeptical of us now appeared friendly, having put us firmly in our place. To say that I was inspired by this session would be an understatement, and I vowed to make a greater effort at improving my flexibility upon my return home. The amount of advanced information relating to *junbi undo* which had been shared was remarkable, and I would later fill many pages with notes and drawings from Hokama *sensei's* lecture.

We returned to the *dojo* a few hours later for evening training with Hokama *sensei*, covering applications from *kururunfa kata* and various other subjects which arose from discussions about the principles and techniques contained within the *kata*. The depth of the explanations and the amount of pain caused through the application of the techniques is quite indescribable, and is something which can only really be appreciated if you have felt it firsthand. Hokama *sensei* specializes in *Kin'na Jutsu*, and most of his *bunkai* contain various restraint holds to finish which result in outrageous amounts of pain for the recipient. Remember how I mentioned about how facing the known can often be more difficult than facing the unknown; well, acting as *uke* for Hokama *sensei* is one such example. Mark was lucky in that he didn't realize how much pain he was about to feel, but for me, I had been here before and knew exactly what to expect. What I wasn't prepared for though, was that Hokama *sensei* was now in better health than he had been during my last visit, and was able to do things faster and more powerfully. Despite this, he appeared to have forgotten what 'tapping out' meant, and would hold a joint lock on almost at the point of breaking whilst you wriggled and screamed for 5 seconds or more. Although this was initially quite funny, after the first few occasions the amusement quickly wore off, and I began to wonder if I had somehow offended him. Various repeated hits and pinches to nerve points, painful finger locks, and an accidental slap to the groin which put me to the *dojo* floor for a good 3 minutes, left my body battered and bruised by the end of the session. Most of the techniques I had been shown were completely lost to me as my mind was elsewhere trying to deal with the pain I was constantly being put in. Quite honestly, it bordered on barbaric, and I was not particularly happy about it at the time. I left the session hoping that it had all been a test of some kind to see if I was serious and sincere, but I was left with a nagging feeling in the back of my mind that something wasn't quite right.

## **Endure!**

After another hefty breakfast courtesy of Mrs Hokama, we made our way down to the *dojo* for morning training. This morning we would be concentrating upon *Kobudo* and in particular, the *Bo* and *Nunchaku*. Practice began with the basic 2-Man *kumi bo kata*, steadily increasing the pace until we were attacking each other in a more realistic manner. Such training serves to hone the senses due to the element of danger being increased greatly by the presence of weapons.

A number of close range applications were then covered, using postures from the classical *kata* of *Goju Ryu* to perform various joint locks and takedowns in order to disarm the opponent of their weapon. A number of techniques were also covered which used the *Bo* to crush the fingers or toes of the opponent which were extremely painful! Although Hokama *sensei's* main *kobudo* teacher was Matayoshi Shinpo *sensei*, his *kobudo* has a very different feel to it than the *Matayoshi Ryu*, and incorporates techniques from many different lineages, particularly *Yamane Ryu* as Hokama *sensei's* grandfather was a student of Oshiro Chojo.

Single and double *nunchaku* were also practiced, including some very unique ways of using double *nunchaku* with one hand which were completely new to me and very interesting. This method generated a tremendous amount of power, and also served as a form of *hojo undo* for that particular weapon. Such ideas would once have been the most closely guarded secret of somebody long forgotten to time. To be presented with the gift of such a treasure was a great feeling and much appreciated. During the times when I wasn't screaming in pain, and more

capable of absorbing the lessons being presented, I was quite overwhelmed with the amount of knowledge which is retained by Hokama *sensei*. This understanding extends well past the barriers of styles, and it quickly became apparent how *karate* consists of a multitude of universal principles which can be applied in various contexts. Despite its apparent complexity, *karatedo* is actually quite simple and direct once the fundamental principles are understood and you are able to apply them to all techniques. Once this is achieved it is possible to see the shared links between all forms of martial arts, regardless of style or country of origin.

Following morning training we spoke at length over more *bubishi* tea about herbal medicines and injury treatment in relation to martial arts. Hokama *sensei* is a practitioner of Traditional Chinese Medicine and regularly uses acupuncture, cupping and herbal remedies in order to heal injuries sustained through training. Such information, it was explained to us, was common knowledge in the old days for medical treatment was too expensive for most people. Because of this, many families understood about medicine and the knowledge was passed down through generations. Hokama *sensei* went on to show us some of the injuries he had sustained over the years as a result of practice including the loss of his front teeth through *kumite* in high school, and a nasty scar in his abdomen caused by stabbing himself with a *sai*. He explained that his family couldn't afford to have his injuries treated professionally at the time so they were left to heal naturally.

Barrett *sensei's* luggage had arrived that morning so in between training sessions, Mark and I travelled to *Tomari* to hand it to him. This allowed us an opportunity to chat for a while and catch up on what everybody had been up to. Barrett *sensei* was training at the *Jundokan dojo* of his teacher Miyazato Eiichi *sensei* during our stay, and it was the first time that he had returned to the *dojo* since the passing of his teacher. It was great swapping accounts for an hour, and we all arranged to meet up the following day at

Shuri castle where we could spend the afternoon doing some sightseeing together.

Returning back to the *dojo*, Mark and I trained again with Hokama *sensei*, this time focusing upon *kata* application. Various topics were covered including animal styles, drunken fist, *kin'na*, *kyusho*, the use of hardness and softness, and how *Sanchin* and *Tensho* principles are used to augment applications from the classical *kata*. The amount of information imparted and the amount of pain caused was quite astounding, but I'm afraid that many of the finer details were completely lost on me for I was unable to concentrate due to the amount of hurt which was being inflicted upon me. I can quite honestly admit that I was on edge for the vast majority of the session, and my training notes reflect that I remembered very little of the wealth of information that was imparted by Hokama *sensei*. I thought this was a great shame, and I was frustrated at myself for allowing so many negative feelings to creep in during the session to distract from the useful information which was being shared. Looking back in hindsight it is easy to admonish myself that I should have been stronger, but at the time this was extremely difficult. I have been struck extremely hard in the past in boxing matches, MMA, and real life encounters. I've been knocked unconscious, hit with bottles, bricks, metal poles, had my nose broken several times, broken numerous teeth, even been set on fire; but none of this compared at all to what Hokama *sensei* could do. It was literally like being Tasered or electrocuted, and in truth it terrified me every time he wanted to demonstrate something.

That evening as I sat down to write my training notes I seriously began to wonder what had I let myself in for this time. My body was already feeling quite battered, and I was only two days into the trip! Putting these thoughts aside I settled down to get some rest, ready for the group training session tomorrow. I also had my fingers tightly crossed that my luggage might finally arrive so that I could change into some clean clothes!

## **Group Training**

In the morning, Mark and I met with Barrett *sensei* at the famous Shuri gate. The weather was bright and sunny for the first time since we had arrived, and it was shaping up to be a very pleasant day indeed. We arrived a few minutes early, so I took the opportunity to grab a quick drink from a vending machine. Whilst I was putting in my coins and selecting a bottle of Iced Tea, Barrett *sensei* sneaked up from behind and launched his ambush attack. Luckily, my *ninja* instinct served me well and I was able to skillfully evade his strike without spilling a drop. I joked that he must be getting old and immediately knew that I would pay for that comment at some point in the future when *sensei* would be grinning and laughing whilst I struggled to perform another set of cat stretches!

Although out of season, the castle grounds were busy with visitors from all over the world and there was plenty going on to stir the senses. We

spent the morning wandering around discussing the architecture and gardening styles, picking up plenty of ideas to play with on our return home. Most of the time I spend with my *sensei* is in a training type environment, so it was a really nice opportunity to just spend a day together as a group chatting about life, *karate*, and enjoying the warm sunshine. Being out of season, a lot of the castle buildings were under restoration, covered with scaffolding which spoiled the view slightly. This would be worth it though for the many tourists who flock to the island during the summer period, helping to provide jobs and a boost to the local economy. The grounds appear much older these days, and look much more dignified now that the fresh paint has worn a little. It's easy to allow the imagination to wander and think about the many past *karate* greats who would have walked along these very same paths. This is what is so special about visiting the island of *karate*.

After a quick lunch of Octopus Gyoza and an ice cream, we made our way toward the *Kinjo* stone pavement, and a little sacred grove off to the side of it which was once a secluded training area for the local *Shurite* masters. Inside this grove (*utaki*) are some magnificent Banyan trees which are probably older than *karate* itself. It is easy to imagine the countless repetitions of *kata* which must have been conducted over the top of their great roots. We spent some time breathing in the air and feeling the soil, using the great trees to enhance the breathing exercises of

Miyagi *sensei's junbi undo*. I wondered if he too took the opportunity to stop here during his run up the *Kinjo* path?

Continuing our way down to the bottom of the *Kinjo* pavement, my stomach began to knot, for I knew what was about to come. As we reached the bottom, Barrett *sensei* asked us to hand over our bags to him, and we were then instructed to run back up the pavement all the way to the top. There are many *karateka* all over the world who will be familiar with this stretch of road, and can appreciate the challenge it presents. For those who don't know, the *Kinjo* pavement is over 500 years old and is actually a staircase which runs from the *Kinjo* River, up a steep hill to the walls of *Shuri* Castle. The climb gets progressively steeper, quickly sapping the energy of the legs and the oxygen from the lungs. The same climb formed part of Miyagi Chojun *sensei's* daily endurance run in his younger years, and he regularly used to send his students up it as part of a 'warm up'. Mark and I ran to the top to the great amusement of the passing tourists who were passing in the opposite direction. On a number of occasions, the path veers around to the right which prevents you from seeing how far you have left to go. This psychological factor makes the climb even more difficult. By the time we arrived at the top I was covered with sweat and breathing heavily under the warm sun. I really hoped that our luggage would arrive today as my clothes were now in a terrible state! Even the mosquitos were avoiding me.

The afternoon was over far too quickly, and we said our goodbyes until the following day as Mark and I returned to the *Kenshikan* for the evening group training.

The children's class at Hokama *sensei's dojo* began at 6pm amid an amazing display of *nunchaku* skills from children as young as 4 years old! The kids were really impressive as they sped their way through *karate* and *kobudo kata*, along with *bunkai*, with a seriousness and dedication which would put most adult practitioners to shame. Hokama *sensei* makes a point of making the children's lessons fun, with a view of boosting their confidence, for he said that the Japanese education system can often be quite stifling to a child's personal development in a society which frowns upon outgoing behavior. At the end of the lesson, the personal accomplishments of various children in the fields of education, sports, and culture were praised in front of the group, with each child receiving a loud applause. There was also time dedicated to math and language studies covering English, Spanish, German and Chinese. The children were nothing short of brilliant, and the respect which is given to Hokama *sensei* from their parents is 100% deserved. It was especially nice to see many of the same faces I had met at the *dojo* 3 years earlier still practicing hard and progressing in their *karate* with enthusiasm. It fills me with great optimism for the future.

The adult's class began at 8pm, and students began arriving from 7pm onwards to work on their own personal training. This gave me a chance to catch up with some old friends and to make a few new ones. I was especially pleased to see Senaha Hiroshi *san* again and remembered him fondly from my previous visit for his strong *ude kitae*. Senaha *san* explained to me that he had suffered a neck injury which resulted in him being temporarily paralyzed a short time ago. Whilst in hospital he had *dojo* members bring various *hojo undo* equipment to him so that he could train from his bed. Doctors feared that he would never walk again, but Senaha *san* trained hard to recover his health, teaching himself to operate again by using different nerves and muscle groups. Now back training

regularly at the *dojo*, Senaha *san* wakes every day at 4am to conduct an 8km walk/jog, 7 days a week! Senaha *san* is also 65 years old!!!!!!! I was astonished by this story and full of admiration. Senaha *san* explained that he thought *karate* was very good for the health, and this is why he practices. I think we could all learn heaps from Senaha *san's* determination and bravery.

The group session began with *junbi undo*, quickly followed by various body conditioning drills. The level of conditioning at the *Kenshikan* is very high and students can be seen regularly hitting everything within arm's reach whilst they perform various exercises. For *Ude Kitae* I paired with an 18 year old youth called Kiwabi *san*, who had been training for just 2 years. I was so impressed with his level of conditioning, and still had bruising to my arm some two weeks later. I watched Kiwabi *san* closely for the remainder of the lesson and was greatly impressed by his ability and attitude to training. A natural athlete with a strong high school baseball record, Kiwabi *san* is destined for great things if he continues with such spirit. The group training sessions always provide a hard workout with a great atmosphere of group endeavor. Everybody helps one another and there are no egos among the students of various ages. Bruised and battered by the end of the session, I was grinning ear to ear with the feeling of accomplishment which you can only get through undergoing such training. Although *karate* is for the most part a solitary pursuit, group training sessions like this forge strong bonds through shared endeavor, and it is a great thing to experience this.

Best of all, our luggage had now arrived!!!!!!

## The Tour

Today our whole group got together to attend the '*karate* history tour' with Hokama *sensei* and his student Taira *san*. This is an absolute must for any visitor to Okinawa who has even the slightest interest into the history of *karate*, and the persons responsible for its development.
A very important thing in *budo* is the concept of *giri*, or obligation. As followers of a tradition, it is correct behavior to give thanks to those who dedicated their lives to developing and passing along the art through the generations so that it can enrich our lives in the present day. The *karate* tour which is organized by Hokama *sensei* is tailored to the individual requirements of the group, and the sites visited will reflect the lineage of the style practiced by those attending. As *Goju Ryu* practitioners, our day would be spent visiting the tombs of the masters found in our particular lineage, and other areas of historical significance with regards to the development of *karate* in general. This would provide us with an opportunity to kneel before their tombs to offer a simple thank you and to learn more about the history and culture which influenced the direction of the Ryukyu martial traditions. I should stress that without going on the tour organized by Hokama *sensei* this would have been extremely difficult, even if the locations of the tombs were marked on a map. Another thing to consider is what gets missed by simply not knowing, for example in 2003 I managed to locate the monument

dedicated to Itosu Anko but had no idea that it was actually stood in front of Itosu *sensei's* tomb. Also unknown to me at the time was the fact that the tombs of *Bushi* Matsumura and Hanashiro Chomo were in the same graveyard. The great thing about having Hokama *sensei* lead the tour is that he provides an excellent commentary throughout in English, providing an in-depth historical background for each of the sites visited. This greatly enhances the experience and also provides the opportunity to ask questions.

Our first stop was at the Ryukyu Archaeological Centre in Nishihara, which Hokama *sensei* introduced it as 'his office'. The museum is a little off the beaten track from the more popular museums located in Shuri, but there are some great exhibits there which demonstrate the rich natural history of the Ryukyu islands going back thousands of years. Crude weapons and hunting tools fashioned from seashells and sharks teeth can be found amongst the displays, as well as examples of ancient pottery, tools, jewelry, and exhibits which show the ancient architecture of the indigenous inhabitants. The fact that such a small island has such a rich and diverse history has always amazed me, and it was great to learn a little more about this relatively unknown side of Okinawa. From here, we headed toward *Ginowan* and the tomb of Miyagi Chojun *sensei*, founder of the *Goju Ryu*, and a legend in the Okinawan martial arts. Pulling into the car park area directly behind the tomb, Hokama *sensei* pointed out a couple of small caves carved into the hard rock by the side of the road. These, he explained, were used by Japanese soldiers during the battle of Okinawa, and were dotted along pretty much every elevated position in the area. These sustained heavy bombing prior to the Americans landing, and I can only imagine how terrifying it must have been for the soldiers making the climb up such hills. Turning my attention in the opposite direction toward the ocean, I saw the sprawling concrete landscape that Okinawa had become and wondered how much Miyagi *sensei's* view had changed over the years. His tomb was as well maintained as ever, and I respectfully knelt before him once again to offer a word of thanks for his efforts in developing *Goju Ryu* so that I could enjoy it today. Although more familiar to me this time, I was still struck by the imposing atmosphere which seems to surround the tomb as you approach it. It feels as though you are being watched and is quite difficult to accurately describe. Despite the intense experience, I really enjoy visiting this tomb, and am always relaxed by the stunning view of the ocean that it affords.

From here we headed down toward *Shuri* to visit the tombs of *Bushi* Matsumura, Itosu Anko, and Hanashiro Chomo. This gravesite always struck me as kind of odd, feeling as though it is placed in the middle of a housing estate and shouldn't really be there. Located near to the *Shiritsu Byoin* monorail station, the plots of land where the tombs are located were gifts from the Ryukyu king to *Bushi* Matsumura and Itosu Anko in reward for their services to the government.

Next we headed further south to the beautiful *Shikinaen*, where we had an opportunity to explore by ourselves and share lunch. The old summer residence of the Ryukyu royal family was also the home of *Bushi* Matsumura during the later years of his life, and the area where he taught *Te* techniques to the King. The grounds of the summer residence were also the site of a fierce battle where Urasoe Choshi *Udun's* three sons took revenge against the Shimazu *samurai* on 7th May 1609 in response to him being taken hostage. They entered the grounds

in secret and attacked a number of Shimazu *samurai*, killing two of their officers before they themselves were slain.

The grounds of *Shikinaen* are a serene oasis of calm in the middle of the business of *Naha*, which has become an ever expanding maze of concrete. Sitting on the open veranda of the residence, looking out over the large pond toward the Chinese style tea house and the stone bridge, I enjoyed a few peaceful moments alone, reflecting upon the direction of my training. Mark was running around taking millions of photographs, inspired by the garden design for future projects he could do back home. Mark is a very skilled landscape gardener who specializes in water features and pond design, so he was like a kid in a sweetshop! I made my way over the stone bridge toward the tea house and caught up with Barrett *sensei* and Clarke *sensei* who were enjoying a quiet chat whilst taking in the view. We soon caught up with Hokama *sensei*, and shared a lunch which consisted of some very tasty Okinawan dishes and some rather odd ones which caused much laughter from Taira *san* as my face contorted against the overpowering sourness of whatever it was I had been 'convinced' to try. This is as much a part of the experience of Okinawa as is training in the *dojo*, and has provided me many great memories and stories over the years;

you just have to pluck up the courage to try new things, even when you know you're being tricked!

Following lunch we were back in the cars and heading West of *Shuri*, toward the grounds of *Bengadake* where the founder of *Shotokan*, Funakoshi Gichin *sensei*, would spend many a quiet moment composing poetry and practicing *karate* in peace. This was a first for me, and I was somewhat pleasantly surprised that the temple was still there, for I had mistakenly assumed that it had been destroyed like most other historically important places in the area. A little further down the road from *Bengadake* was the tomb of Higashionna Kanryo *sensei*, teacher of the founder of Goju Ryu, Miyagi Chojun *sensei*, and one of the most legendary figures of 19th century *toudi*. This is one of those spots which you would be unlikely to find on a map without local knowledge of the area, and this is probably the main reason why the tomb is rarely visited by *Goju Ryu* practitioners, even in Okinawa. The long grass and somewhat overgrown foliage surrounding the tomb is home of many a poisonous *habu* snake, and this adds somewhat to the feeling that you shouldn't really be there. I wrote before about how although imposing, Miyagi *sensei's* tomb is quite welcoming whereas the tomb of Higashionna *sensei* feels more intimidating. I don't know if this is something in my own imagination, but it feels real enough to me to notice. I think this tomb is a real treasure, and up until a few years ago I had no idea it still existed. The opportunity to pay my respects once again to this great teacher was much appreciated.

Staying with *Nahadi* history for a while, we headed back into downtown *Naha* toward *Matsuyama Koen* and *Fukushuen*. During the drive I enquired with Hokama *sensei* regarding the whereabouts of Aragaki Seisho's tomb, but Hokama *sensei* regretfully informed me that despite many years of searching he had been unable to locate it thus far, fearing it may have been destroyed during the battle of Okinawa. Along the route he did however point out the tomb of *Toudi* Sakugawa, but we didn't have time to stop here unfortunately. Again, I was amazed that this still existed and this raised an interesting question in my mind regarding claims that he had died in Beijing. We arrived at *Matsuyama Koen* and spent some time hearing Hokama *sensei* lecture about the amazing history of the grounds and how the landscape had changed since the days when various practitioners would gather with the Chinese visitors in order to learn from each other. Back then, the hill was 20 meters higher and covered with tall pine trees, hence the name *Matsuyama* (Pine Mountain). The relentless bombing of *Naha* resulted in dramatic changes to the landscape, and the park now looks nothing like it would have back then. Hokama *sensei* explained how many people would gather here, each bringing whatever training equipment or weapons they had at home, along with some lunch, and everybody would exchange ideas and enjoy training together. What a wonderful sight that must have been, and for young Higashionna *sensei* who lived just across the street, what an introduction to his native martial tradition. Is it little wonder that he was inspired enough to make the epic journey to Fuzhou at such a young age to further his training? Again, we were left to our own devices for a while to explore the grounds of *Fukushuen*. This is a place I visit frequently whenever I am in Okinawa and is another little oasis of calm and a nice escape from busy *Naha*. Constructed to celebrate the close historical ties between Okinawa and *Fuzhou*, the structures and gardening styles within are representative of those found in *Fuzhou*, and are what Higashionna *sensei* would have been familiar with during his stay. Once again, Mark was a man possessed with his camera, and who could blame him!

Back in the vehicles, we followed the coastline toward *Tomari*, passing the International Cemetery and the monument to Admiral Perry, toward an ancient gravesite and the birthplace of *Tomaridi*. The old style turtleback tomb and the large open space in front, surrounded by high walls and coastal cliffs provided the ultimate secret training area for the warriors of *Tomari*. The walls provided natural *hojo undo* tools with which to strengthen the legs by performing various jumping exercises which we were encouraged to try for ourselves. A large gap between walls also provided a means of strengthening ones *Shiko Dachi* by straddling the two walls and performing punches. My legs seemed to have shrunk since my

last visit as I no longer could seem to hold my balance and fell repeatedly. Luckily it wasn't caught on camera…..or was it? I will be paying Mike Clarke *sensei* off for many years in order to prevent the footage from becoming public! We followed the narrow path further down toward the coastline and came to the entrance of *Furuherin*, where the Chinese master *Channan* would take refuge upon becoming shipwrecked off the coast of *Tomari*. Although rather unfortunate for *Channan*, this was a great bit of luck for the practitioners of *Tomari*, who in return for their kindness toward him were rewarded with tuition in Chinese *kempo* which greatly enhanced their martial traditions and elevated the reputation of the Tomari *Bushi*. Our tour of Tomari was completed with a visit to the monument erected in honour of its most famous master, *Bushi* Matsumora, who famously defeated a Satsuma samurai by disarming him of his sword and throwing it into the *Asato* River. This is another monument which I think should be elsewhere as it always seemed somewhat neglected and dirty.

We returned to the vehicles and headed South towards *Tomigusuku* and the tomb of Miyazato Eiichi *sensei*. Prior to leaving for Okinawa, Barrett *sensei* asked if I could help to arrange a visit to Miyazato *sensei's* tomb so that he could pay his respects. This was an obligation which I took extremely seriously, and I was anxious to be successful for him, to the point of becoming a bit of a pest during the day by repeatedly reminding Hokama *sensei* so that he wouldn't forget. Arriving in *Tomigusuku* I began to worry as neither Hokama *sensei* nor Taira *san* could remember where the tomb was located! I remembered that the tomb stood on the edge of a hill and wasn't actually part of a gravesite, so would be particularly difficult to find. We made a number of wrong turns, Hokama *sensei* made a number of phone calls, and much to my relief we were finally able to locate the tomb. I carefully kept myself in the background here to allow my *sensei* and Clarke *sensei* the opportunity to pay their respects to their teacher, and I felt a nice sense of pride having played a small part in helping my teacher and his friend. This was one of the most important parts of the trip for me. Barrett *sensei* and Clarke *sensei* had a quiet chat together in front of Miyazato *sensei's* tomb, and upon observing this; Hokama *sensei* said to me "this is the meaning of *Giri*". Early on in the day, Hokama *sensei* asked "why does your teacher train at the *Jundokan*, but you train with me?" This was one of those awkward questions which I had been expecting to come up at some point and I tactfully explained to Hokama *sensei* that my teacher continued to train at the *Jundokan* out of a sense of *Giri* to his teacher Miyazato *sensei*. Hokama *sensei* was pleased at this answer and replied "your teacher is a good man". He then began to sing a *Yakuza* song about *Giri* which greatly amused Taira *san* who went on to jokingly inform me that Hokama *sensei* is the leader of the *Yakuza*.

## A Surprise Meeting

Following the tour we returned to the *Kenshikan* where we spent some time looking around the museum as a group. Hokama *sensei* also brushed a number of calligraphy's for everybody present, giving us some great souvenirs to take back with us to our homes and *dojo*. Whilst looking around the museum, I saw a photograph of Kinjo Seikichi *sensei* attached to an older group photograph of Miyagi Chojun *sensei* and senior students. I asked Hokama *sensei* whether Kinjo *sensei* was in this picture and he confirmed that he was, pointing him out to me in the back row of the photograph. I was really happy to learn this fact, but I was about to become a whole lot happier. I said to Hokama *sensei* that Kinjo *sensei* had previously spoken to me about his training with Miyagi *sensei*, and that I had always wanted to speak with him further about the subject but did not know where to find him as he was no longer a member of the *Jundokan*. Hokama *sensei* disappeared briefly before returning with his list of contacts. Kinjo *sensei* was not in there, so he then telephoned the directory to try to find him. He said that this probably wouldn't work as Kinjo is a very common name in Okinawa. Still, the thought was there, and I was extremely grateful for his help, but only a few moments later, Hokama *sensei* was speaking loudly on the phone and making arrangements to meet somebody. Perhaps we might get a lead on Kinjo *sensei's* whereabouts and be able to contact him for the next time if we were lucky. Following the phone call, Hokama *sensei* thrust a piece of paper into my hand with an address scribbled on it in Japanese and then said we had to go there for 7pm that evening to meet Kinjo *sensei* himself. Cue the first use of the line 'this can't be happening!' Everything became quite surreal from this point, and I must admit to feeling quite panicked, especially when I discovered that Hokama *sensei* was not coming with us! There was no time to dwell though, for we had an appointment to keep. Taira *san* returned in his Taxi and drove us to the address scribbled on the piece of paper by Hokama *sensei*. Arriving in plenty of time, I quickly ran into a supermarket to buy some fruit and cakes, for it would have been bad manners to have turned up empty handed, and as I exited the store I saw an elderly gentlemen on the opposite side of the road, smiling and beckoning us over.

Before I left for Okinawa I had a list of things which I wanted to achieve during the trip. At the very top of this list was meeting Kinjo Seikichi *sensei* once again. I have some wonderful memories of training with Kinjo *sensei*, and before I had ever met him I knew who he was due to the amount of respect given to him by my teacher. Barrett *sensei* used to always tell me about this nice little old man at the *Jundokan* who could completely control you during *kakie* in a very subtle way which left you wondering how he did it. A few years later I was to feel this for myself.

On my first visit to the *Jundokan* I had the great fortune to have been taught almost exclusively by Yasuda *sensei* and Kinjo *sensei* who would arrive at the *dojo* on alternate days at 5pm to teach me for a couple of hours. Up until the final two days of my first visit I hadn't even known that Kinjo *sensei* was a direct student of Miyagi *sensei*. I had found a rare photograph of what I thought was Miyagi *sensei* in a book and I showed this to Kinjo *sensei*, asking him if he could confirm whether it was him or not? Kinjo *sensei* said "that is my teacher" and my heart skipped a beat in excitement. A few years later I spent more time with Kinjo *sensei*, and got the chance to speak to him about his experiences as a student of the founder. I have some great memories of certain corrections in *Seisan* which were given along with his memories about how Miyagi *sensei* would apply this technique against his students. He used to call me 'baby champion' because I looked so young, and I can't describe how much I had enjoyed learning from him. The last time I had seen him was at the 50th Anniversary party for the *Jundokan*, and I remembered how he seemed to be stood on his own for most of the night whilst the other seniors were surrounded by various 'important people' from overseas. For some reason this made me feel very sad. I could also identify with him somewhat that night as I had not been told about this party, and had turned up wearing shorts and sandals whilst everyone else was in dinner suits. Finding myself in a corner of the banqueting hall with Kinjo *sensei*, I thanked him for all of his help and he simply smiled and said "next time". Following my return to the UK there was a split between the *Jundokan* and the *Kyokai*, with many of the seniors leaving with the *Kyokai*. Kinjo *sensei* remained for a time with the *Jundokan,* but I learned some time later that he also left the *dojo* and became part of the *Kyokai*. He soon also left the *Kyokai* and I had heard nothing more of him since. I had given up hope of ever training with him again. Now, stood once more before Kinjo *sensei*, I couldn't help smiling and thanking my lucky stars that I had the opportunity to spend some more time in the company of this wonderful *karateka*.

Kinjo *sensei* led the way up to his apartment and ushered us into his home where we were greeted by his wife. He appeared quite frail and his characteristic shake seemed more pronounced than the last time I had seen him. Barrett *sensei* and I exchanged worried looks and agreed that we wouldn't stay very long, just a quick cup of tea and we would excuse ourselves and leave him in peace. We sat around his dining room table and almost immediately Kinjo *sensei* turned the subject of conversation to *karate*. He told us that he had been a student of Miyagi Chojun *sensei* for 4 years, training at the famous garden *dojo*. The many years that had passed since the death of his teacher had not dulled his impression of him and Kinjo *sensei* entertained us with many stories about his teacher and fond memories of the training. Quite without warning, Kinjo *sensei* then stood up and began to perform various *junbi undo* exercises, relating them to *Sanchin kata*. He then began to perform the breathing exercises of *junbi undo* and I swear it was like watching a different person. As cliché as this may sound, Kinjo *sensei* suddenly appeared many years younger than he was. I was greatly impressed by his movements, and particularly his use of breathing which echoed through the small room. Kinjo *sensei* clearly didn't remember any of us and asked about our backgrounds. Clarke *sensei* and Barrett *sensei* informed him that they were students of the late Miyazato Ei'ichi *sensei*. I said to Kinjo *sensei* how we all remembered his great ability at *kakie* and how much we had enjoyed training with him some years ago. Upon hearing this, Kinjo *sensei* apologized, saying that his arms were no longer very strong. Immediately after this he stood up again and asked me if I would mind practicing *kakie* with him. I was overjoyed and made exactly the same mistake that I had done all those years ago, the same mistake that Barrett *sensei* had also made even longer ago. Fooled by his appearance once again, I took it easy. Kinjo *sensei* pushed back with the force of a young man, and I responded naturally by having to use more energy to move his arm which was by now locked firmly into position. Over-exerting myself, Kinjo *sensei* sensed this and quickly switched from *Go* to *Ju* to unbalance me, throwing in an arm bar to help me on my way as I bounced against his wall from the momentum. I was grinning from ear to ear and caught Clarke *sensei's* eye who simply smiled and said "enjoy". I could not believe that I was practicing *kakie* again with Kinjo *sensei*. I was so happy. We sat back down at the table and I was pleased to see that Kinjo *sensei* was also smiling and seemed to be enjoying our surprise visit.

Thinking that we had taken up enough of Kinjo *sensei's* time, we began to make preparations to say goodbye, but before this was possible, Kinjo *sensei's* wife began cooking up a heap of food which could have fed a *dojo* full of visitors. We would be going nowhere for quite some time it appeared. Each time we tried to leave them in peace, Mrs Kinjo would make another batch of food! We were beginning to feel quite guilty. I got up from the table and quietly explained to Mrs Kinjo while she was cooking that she really didn't have to worry about us, and that we didn't want to inconvenience her any further. Hearing this, she took it to mean that we didn't like the current dishes, so she then began preparing something different!!! We really couldn't believe this was all happening, but what a great way to spend an evening in Okinawa. The hospitality and kindness of Kinjo *sensei* and his wife was beyond words and I am so grateful for their time. I can honestly say that this was one of the best experiences of my time in *karate* and I don't think my writing can ever accurately explain what we all felt that evening.

As we prepared to leave, Kinjo *sensei* had one more surprise up his sleeve………..

Kinjo *sensei* asked if we would like to meet him at 10am the following day at the *Budokan* for training. We all looked at each other and couldn't quite believe that we had heard correctly. I double checked a number of times, and yes, it was quite certain, Kinjo *sensei* was offering to teach us the following morning. We of course agreed to this, very excited about the opportunity to train with him once again, for we all believed that this would no longer be possible due to a number of factors. Kinjo *sensei* went on to say that he would take us through the same type of training session which Miyagi Chojun *sensei* used to hold at his garden *dojo*. Although I was ecstatic at the opportunity that had presented itself, I was also worried about what Hokama *sensei* would say about this. Our training out there had not been structured and there were no set times for when we were supposed to be training with him, I also didn't know what plans he had made for the next day. I explained this to Kinjo *sensei* and asked if he could call Hokama *sensei* to check that it would be ok with him. Kinjo *sensei* picked up the phone and called Hokama *sensei*, speaking with him for a couple of minutes in excited tones, smiling at us the whole time. He appeared to be genuinely happy at the chance to train again. Suddenly he thrust the telephone toward me saying that Hokama *sensei* wanted to speak with me. I answered the phone and immediately heard Hokama *sensei* saying sharply "when are you leaving?" I replied that we were about to leave and he abruptly ended the call. I handed the telephone back to Kinjo *sensei*, thanking him, but was now overcome with a sense of impending doom. Barrett *sensei* asked if everything was ok and I didn't really know what to say, I just said that I would make things right that evening.

Leaving Kinjo *sensei* and his wife, we made our way back to our lodgings in a state of disbelief. This whole turn of events had been quite unexpected and was certainly something which we couldn't have planned for prior to leaving for Okinawa. This would be a once in a lifetime experience, but I just hoped that everything would turn out ok and that I hadn't accidently caused offence to Hokama *sensei*. I would have never considered for one moment asking Kinjo *sensei* to teach us; he had excitedly volunteered this of himself, and I deeply regretted that my command of Japanese was not good enough to explain fully my concerns. I also did not want to offend Kinjo *sensei* by declining the opportunity he had so generously offered. I had inadvertently allowed myself to be put in a position where my next actions could have a really bad impact upon a number of people who I cared about deeply, and I was not comfortable about it at all.

During the journey home, I don't think I said more than two words to Mark as I was quite lost in my own thoughts, trying to figure out how I was going to fix the situation. Upon our arrival at the *dojo*, I told Mark to go back to the room and I went upstairs to Hokama *sensei's* home. I rang the doorbell and a few moments later, Hokama *sensei* appeared wearing a *kimono*, which for some reason made me even more nervous. I explained how Kinjo *sensei* had asked us all to train with him tomorrow morning at the *Budokan* and apologized that my Japanese had not been good enough to explain properly to him how I would need to check first. I said that I really hoped that my actions had not caused a problem for him. Hokama *sensei* went quiet for a while and then said "yes, big problem". Oh no........! Hokama *sensei* explained that three important men from Russia were coming tomorrow and that I had to meet them when they arrived at the *dojo*. A high ranking member of the *Kyokushinkai* would also be arriving tomorrow and in the evening he was going to visit Shinjo Kiyohide *sensei* of the *Uechi Ryu*. This was all news to me and had not been mentioned at all up until that point. I explained to Hokama *sensei* that I was sorry for causing a problem, that I would remain at the *dojo* with him as requested, and that Mark would deliver the message to the rest of the group saying that I couldn't attend. I was truly saddened. Hokama *sensei* said that this was no good as I had made an agreement. In truth, I had absolutely no idea what I was supposed to do or say at this point. Once again I apologized and bowed my head low. Hokama *sensei* returned inside and I went back down to my room and spoke with Mark for a while, trying to figure the situation out. I decided that I would speak with Hokama *sensei* again in the morning and try to do a better job of explaining after he had calmed down. The fantastic events of the day had been spoilt somewhat by this incident, and I felt extremely disappointed to say the least. I still don't really understand what I could have done to make it better. As a student of Barrettt *sensei*, I've become quite accustomed to looking for the hidden lessons within every situation, but for the life of me I still can't figure this one out.

## An Unforgettable Experience

After a sleepless night, I awoke early and got everything in order before Hokama *sensei* woke. I didn't know what to expect so I made sure that my bags were packed in case we were asked to leave the *dojo*. Poor old Mark was trying everything he could think of to help me, even offering to stay behind and meet the Russian men, but I explained that this was my problem and it would be ok. Hokama *sensei* called us upstairs for breakfast and seemed like a different person to the previous night. He asked if we had enjoyed our evening and enquired about Kinjo *sensei*, asking how he was. I was dumbfounded, and more than a little confused. He said that the Russian men were arriving late in the afternoon and that they were leaders of *Goju Ryu* in their country. He told us how they would be flying him out to Moscow later that year for a seminar but that they always cause him many problems as they never keep to their word, telling us that he wasn't even sure if they were even coming today. I sat quite quietly through breakfast, trying my best to make sense of things. I again approached the subject of training Kinjo *sensei* that morning and he seemed very happy, telling us to enjoy ourselves. We finished our breakfast and were cheerfully sent on our way by Hokama *sensei*. Walking down to the bus stop I looked at Mark and we both asked "what was that all about?"

We arrived early at the *Budokan* by monorail and met up with Barrett *sensei*, Clarke *sensei* and Mitch. They enquired if everything was ok, and I told them about the events of the previous evening. Barrett *sensei* wondered if there had been some confusion and whether Hokama *sensei* thought we had inconvenienced Kinjo *sensei* by asking him to teach us, fearing for his relatives' health. I was still deeply troubled by it and as 10am came and went with no sign of Kinjo *sensei*, I began to worry even more. What if *I* had misunderstood? What if I got the wrong day? What if I misheard the time? What if Kinjo *sensei* regretted what he said and had changed his mind? What if he had forgotten? What if he was unwell? Seeing my concern, Barrett *sensei* took me aside and had a quiet word with me to help allay my fears. Funny how some things stick in your head, but I can remember every tiny detail about that morning and as I write this now, one year later, it feels as though it was only yesterday.

About 15 minutes later, I saw Kinjo *sensei* tottering toward the *Budokan*, dressed smartly and with a rucksack on his back. I rushed to meet him and help him with his bags, and he immediately apologized for being late, saying that there had been a problem with the bus. I couldn't believe that he had taken the bus and wished that we had been more thoughtful in helping him travel. As a group we rushed around to pay Kinjo *sensei's* entrance fee, carry his bags, and hold open doors; trying our best to help the morning progress as smoothly as possible for him. As we entered the top floor *dojo* in the *Budokan*, there was an *Aikido* class and a *Kobudo* session already in progress. The *sensei* of both groups stopped to bow and greet Kinjo *sensei*. There was a really nice atmosphere in the *dojo* with people just enjoying their personal training in small groups without any of the nonsense which goes hand in hand with *karate* these days.

After getting changed we bowed in together and were then instructed to form a circle as we began with *junbi undo*. Various technical points were highlighted by Kinjo *sensei*, particularly with regards to the relationship of the exercises with *Sanchin*. Next, we performed *kihon* in a circle with each person counting out ten repetitions as various punches, blocks and kicks which were performed in unison. I should point out that rather than standing in front of the group 'instructing', Kinjo *sensei* was actually doing everything we did, using the opportunity to shed a little sweat! Following this, we were partnered off for blocking practice and I had the good fortune of being Kinjo *sensei's* training partner for the rest of the session. Various combinations of blocks and evasive footwork were practiced and I was struck by the softness of Kinjo *sensei's* blocks, quite unlike the forceful blocking methods now very common within *Goju Ryu*. The strikes were met early along their path and guided off target using timing, circular movement, and blending, in order to draw the opponent in close and cause them to lose balance through their own momentum. The methods relied not upon physical strength, but timing and subtlety, and provided a means by which the defensive methods of *Goju Ryu* could be used by anyone, weak or strong, male or female, young or old. This I believe was in direct contrast to modern methods which are suited only to the strong and able bodied. *Goju Ryu* should be able to be applied by anyone, and I believe this was demonstrated excellently by Kinjo *sensei* who had carried a physical disability for a significant period of his life, yet could still apply his *karate* against strong young men who weren't yet even half his age.

We took a break for water, and Kinjo *sensei* spoke some more about his

training with Miyagi *sensei* and later, with Miyazato Ei'ichi *sensei*, who he followed until his death in 1999. Kinjo *sensei* was eventually to leave the *Jundokan dojo* in the years following the death of his teacher, but his love for *karate* and *Goju Ryu* remained great. I really got the impression that he was enjoying himself that morning, and he stated a number of times how happy he was to be back in a *do-gi*, sweating and practicing.

Following the break we once again partnered up, this time for *kakie* training. Again, I crossed hands with Kinjo *sensei* and had a great time being subtly led and unbalanced by his refined movements. It was like trying to push against a cloud and I constantly found myself either up on my toes or back on my heels, unable to maintain a good grounding. My mind wandered and I smiled at the thought of Kinjo *sensei* doing this many years earlier with Miyagi Chojun *sensei*. Following *kakie* training we all sat on the floor in a single line. One by one we were then called to the front to perform a *kata* in front of the rest of the group. Kinjo *sensei* said that this was how *kata* training was done with Miyagi *sensei* who would sit on a small stool and silently observe, simply grunting loudly if the performance was satisfactory as an indication for the student to leave the floor. As my turn arrived, my heart rate was speeding. As much as I tried to remain calm and composed, the nerves were attacking fiercely, for here I was stood in front of my teacher Barrett *sensei* who always makes me nervous anyway, but on top of that there was also Mike Clarke *sensei* watching closely AND Kinjo *sensei*. I rushed through *Sanseiru* and *Suparinpei*, tensing up far too much and trying to force the movements. Nevertheless, it was a great honour to get the chance to have my *kata* corrected by Kinjo *sensei*. This was also a fortunate moment for me to watch Barrett *sensei* and Clarke *sensei* perform their *kata* too. The whole thing was a once in a lifetime opportunity and a great example of *Ichi Go Ichi E*.

The time passed all too quickly, and we were soon preparing to leave. Barrett *sensei* had a small gift which he had brought from Spain which was wrapped in brown paper. He had brought a number of these with him to Okinawa to hand out to the various friends he met as souvenirs and small tokens of his appreciation. As he offered this to Kinjo *sensei* he immediately protested against it, saying that he wouldn't accept any money. The gift was in a small paper bag which Kinjo *sensei* had mistakenly thought was an envelope containing money. The misunderstanding was explained and Kinjo *sensei* then gratefully accepted the gift. This small episode demonstrated the kind of *karateka* he was. What a great shame there are so few like him. Every action of Kinjo *sensei* over the past 24 hours had reinforced my ideal of what a *karateka* should aim to be, of what every *karateka* **could** be.

We all said our goodbyes and together we collected some money so that we could pay for a taxi to get Kinjo *sensei* home safely. It was my job to see that this happened, but it turned out to be no easy task, for Kinjo *sensei* was insistent upon walking and taking the bus. I explained that it was very hot that day and we had been training for a long time, but Kinjo *sensei* was quite sure, saying that he often walked to *Naminoue* or rode a bicycle. All of the while he was smiling away, and after much persuasion, I managed to get him to agree to taking a taxi on this one occasion. Flagging down a taxi for him, I handed him some money to the driver to pay for the fare home and said my goodbyes. As the taxi drove off down the road with Kinjo *sensei* still smiling out of the window, I felt so grateful to have had the good fortune to have experienced the past 24 hours. Now, rather than my final memory of Kinjo *sensei* being of him stood alone telling me "next time", I could remember us all training together again and him happily waving goodbye as the taxi moved away. As strange as this may seem, I hope in some ways that I never see Kinjo *sensei* again because I don't want to ever change this memory. I hope that he enjoyed himself as much as we all did.

Our group with Kinjo Seikichi sensei at the Budokan

## **Visitors**

Whilst we were in Okinawa we had a very special visitor from mainland Japan come to meet us for a few days. Sue Eddie is a fellow student of Barrett *sensei* who has been residing in Japan for many years. It had been about 10 years since I had last seen her. Sue was instrumental in helping me to arrange my first visit to Okinawa in 2001 by providing a letter of introduction in Japanese to the *Jundokan* and helping to arrange somewhere for me to stay. Despite her best efforts, upon my arrival at the *Minshukan* where I was supposed to be staying, I was told that they no longer had any room for me and that I would have to stay elsewhere. It was 10pm on my first evening in Okinawa and I was 20 years old in a completely alien environment in the middle of *Kokusai Dori* with only my luggage. I frantically spent the next couple of hours trying to find somewhere to change up some travelers cheques so that I could check into a hotel while I figured out what to do. I had no credit cards and no cash, and most hotels turned me away as I only had the traveler's cheques, telling me I would have to wait until the banks opened in the morning. I was terrified at the time, but it all turned out ok in the end and was a great experience to look back on.

Mark and I met everybody in *Kokusai Dori* where we quickly found somewhere to eat lunch together. This gave us all an opportunity to catch up and talk over some delicious traditional Okinawan food. Sue is also a practitioner of *Shiatsu* and a long time student of *Goju Ryu*. She shared some very interesting stories relating to her own training and the ideals of her *sensei* who echoed Kinjo *sensei's* approach with a more *Ju* method of blocking, using timing and circular motion.

Following lunch we walked down to the Chinese Gardens in *Kume*, stopping along the route to buy the obligatory 'Karate Stamps' and to take a look at Nagamine *sensei's Kodokan dojo*. It's amazing that there are still so many old fashioned buildings tucked away in the back streets of *Naha*, seemingly a world away from the modern concrete jungle as it now appears. Looking at the *Kodokan* I tried to imagine what the area would have looked like around the time of its construction. Very difficult to picture whilst stood between the many 6+ story buildings now surrounding it in all directions......I'm sure there's a *karate* analogy hidden in this somewhere.

We spent the rest of the afternoon chatting and relaxing in the tranquil surroundings of *Fukushuen*. Although a little more worn out than I remembered it, I still love the gardens and always spot something new upon each visit.

We said our goodbyes for the day and Mark and I returned to the *Kenshinkan* for the evening group training. Upon our arrival at the *dojo*, I noticed an overwhelming smell of cigarette smoke coming from inside as I opened the door. Bowing upon entry, my attention was drawn to the three 'important visitors' from Russia who were sleeping on the floor in the corner of the *dojo*, with their *do-gi* jackets carelessly strewn across the *dojo* in a mess. Although they had by now been at the *dojo* for a few days, none of them had yet to even glance at Mark or I to acknowledge our existence or say hello, and any of our own attempts to break the ice were met with indifference. This created a very uncomfortable atmosphere. Mark and I went up to our room to change into our *do-gi* ready for the arrival of the children's group.

Following the great fun and organized chaos of the children's class, the adult session once again began with a good sweat session and plenty of conditioning. *Kakie* was also covered, including 2 person through to 5 person *kakie* drills. This was very different to anything I had seen before, but interesting nonetheless. The evenings training played havoc with my already recovering arms and shins which were still heavily bruised from the previous group session and were now quite sore to the touch. I was paired with a particularly strong 40 year old student whose name unfortunately I did not record, but I remember that he was a PE teacher with excellent physical fitness. Each strike was agony! Lost in my own little battle, any thoughts of homesickness, tiredness, or anything else for that matter quickly faded into insignificance for I had only one task to concentrate upon; getting through this bout of *ude kitae*. Just one more, just one more......... Looking over to my right, I was pleased that other members of the *dojo* seemed to be engaged in similar battles with themselves. I was not alone in this regard. As training drew to a close, a number of low tables were laid out in the *dojo* and were quickly piled high

with delicious homemade food and soft drinks. The members of the *Kenshinkan* had decided to throw a welcome feast for their visitors from Russia and England. A small party then followed with everybody giving speeches whilst eating and drinking together.

It was really humbling and I was so pleased that the family atmosphere of the *dojo* had not changed since my last visit. I really enjoyed the group sessions at the *dojo*, probably even more so this time. Maybe it was because it seemed so different from my usual existence in the UK? *Karate* in my life is very much a solitary journey. Of course I have my *sensei*, *sempai's* and students, but the vast majority of my training is done alone. There is nobody else to feed off, no one to help motivate. There is only me, and my own negativity to confront and defeat each time. Rather than feeling sorry for myself, I see this as a blessing for I am presented with a very difficult challenge where the only person I can blame for either my success or failure is myself. If you can succeed whilst stood under the spotlight of only yourself, you can feel confident that you have learnt to be self-sufficient and truly independent. Having said that, when you are then provided with the opportunity to surround yourself briefly with other students who are trying equally hard, you can really appreciate the value of combined effort. To be pushed hard by fellow students who can stretch your limits is also an extremely valuable experience. There are many things about travelling and training in Okinawa which take you completely out of your comfort zone and I would strongly encourage anybody presented with this opportunity to seize it tightly with both hands for it is invaluable.

## **Work To Do**

Mark and I awoke early in the morning to complete a few odd jobs around the *dojo* for Hokama *sensei*. Although this was not asked of us, it is most definitely expected that visitors to the *dojo* should pull their weight, even if it is just ensuring that the tea is prepared and the utensils always cleaned after training. The same thing applies with *Soji* (cleaning the *dojo*). This is never instructed, but Hokama *sensei's* students will always sweep the floor and mop up sweat patches before and during training. Offering to help around the *dojo* is all part of give and take. How rude would it be to turn up at somebody's *dojo* and expect to be taught without repaying this kindness by helping the *sensei*. I would hope that this would be common sense for all visitors, but apparently not.....
Anyway, Mark and I spent the morning trimming the plants around the large gate at the entrance to the *dojo*. To complete this task we were given a pair of shears which were falling to bits, and a rusty old *kama*. I had to smile at this because I was immediately reminded of something Barrett *sensei* had said many years ago about his rickety old straw broom in the corner of his *dojo*. The gist of it was that sometimes we make things a little more difficult just for the sake of being difficult. My students will testify that I too uphold this same tradition. Of course it is easier to clean the floor using a mop, but hey, scooting up and down the *dojo* in the push up position whilst scrubbing is not only fun, it also trains the body and spirit, especially after a hard training session!
Anyway, together Mark and I set about tending to the gate. I had a great time wielding the *kama* about, and viewed it as being cutting practice, a form of *kobudo hojo undo*. I remembered something my friend Asako *san* had told me about her teacher growing up on a farm and becoming very good at cutting with the *kama* through performing work rather than training in the empty air.

Following our chores for the day, we trained in the morning, focusing upon *Bojutsu*. Hokama *sensei* was of course a student of Matayoshi Shinpo *sensei*, but I also discovered that a lot of his ideas concerning the use of the *Bo* came from his grandfather who studied *Shorin Ryu* and *Yamani Ryu Bojutsu* under Oshiro Chojo *sensei*. This was reflected in the application of techniques which utilize sliding hands to rapidly accelerate the *Bo* and cause unpredictability due to the length and range of the weapon constantly changing. Many applications from *Seipai kata* were referenced using the *Bo* to perform various joint locks and takedowns using the postures from the *kata*. It was all very interesting and painful stuff! In particular there was an emphasis upon the *Kosa Dachi* posture in *Seipai* and its various uses for both armed and unarmed techniques.

Following training my friend Geiche took us for lunch at a local Dim Sum restaurant. We had masses of food and left feeling quite full! I had met Geiche by chance in *Shureido* 3 years previous when she was in there enquiring about *Shotokan dojo* in Naha. She was invited to Hokama *sensei's dojo* and now 3 years later she is still living in Okinawa and studying *Goju Ryu* and *Kobudo* at the *Kenshikan*. Not heeding the wisdom of *hara hachibu* (eat until you are only 80% full), Mark and I had eaten far too much, and were now wondering how on earth we would manage to hold it all down during the afternoon training!

Back in the *dojo*, the afternoons training concentrated once again upon various uses for the *Kosa Dachi* from *Seipai*. Special walking methods were covered and then applied to various joint locks and takedowns. This was really interesting for me as it narrowed down the chances for the opponent to escape from the takedowns. *Suiken* or Drunken Fist was also covered from this posture, and we explored ways of rebounding back when our strike had been blocked using unpredictable stepping and loose striking methods. This led onto further discussions about the various animal methods contained in the *Goju Ryu kata*, and I began to see a real similarity to what I had read about *Kojo Ryu* and their use of animal inspired *kamae*. This discussion brought the *kamae* to life and presented a very different idea to me than the still photographs I had seen previously of the postures. Rather than just an interesting side note or piece of history, the animal methods were essential to making the applications work to their most effective.

Following training, Mark and I went into Naha for dinner at a great little 50's diner I remembered from a previous visit in *Kokusai Dori* in 2003. I was delighted to see that it was still there. We also had a well-deserved first beer together in the home of *Goju Ryu*. *Kampai*!!

**Ghosts Of The Past**

For any visitor to Okinawa, it is very important to balance hard training with cultural and historical studies in order to get the most out of your stay. To focus only upon the physical is to miss a major part of what Okinawan *Karate-Do* is all about, and I feel this in part is responsible for the decline in standards over the years. Toward the end of our stay I had planned a short historical tour around the *Kume* area of *Naha* for Mark and Mitch, and then later that day we were to meet up with my friend Geiche again where she would then drive us down to explore the Southern part of the island which I had not seen before.

Meeting early, Mark, Mitch and I headed down to *Naminoue Jingu*, one of my favorite temples on the island. Although a reconstruction, due to the original having been destroyed during WW2, the temple possesses a commanding view of the South China Sea from its position on top of the cliffs. The area around *Naminoue* is now quite famous for its steaks, but just over 100 years ago the area was better known as the center for Confucian and Chinese cultural studies in Okinawa, as well as a meeting place for various Chinese martial artists and members of the *Matsuyama* martial arts study group. In 1846 a Christian missionary called Bettelheim (1811-1870) landed in Okinawa and took over *Gokuku-Ji* which is located next to *Naminoue Jingu*. He banished all Buddhist worshippers and kept the rightful owners of the temple away for the 7 years he occupied the building with his family. Bettelheim was nothing short of a complete nuisance for the Okinawans, and he busied himself in all matters of international affairs between the Ryukyu Kingdom and the rest of the world, despite it having absolutely nothing to do with

him. He also acted as interpreter for Commodore Perry during his big show of strength on the island in 1853. Bettelheim expressed great delight in witnessing the eventual destruction of the temple and made no secret of the fact he despised the Okinawans. Despite this, the local people were forced to remain courteous to him and concede to his many demands. He did all of this not out of a willingness to promote the Christian faith he was supposed to be representing, nor to help open trade links for Western nations with Japan as had been Commodore Perry's aim; he did what he did purely out of a need to boost his own self-importance and take ownership of something which was never his to possess. Over 150 years later I seem to be witnessing similar things still happening on the island.

There is a famous song written by Ronnie Fray called 'The Road To Naminoue' which became something of a hit amongst the American servicemen stationed on the island in the 60's. It has a really haunting sound and I always feel a little sad whenever I hear it. Whilst we walked around the grounds of the temples and the surrounding gardens, I could hear the riff from this song repeating in my head.

Walking down the large stone steps, passing underneath the large *Shinto Torii* gate, we next stopped by the *Tenpi Jingu*. The *Tenpi* complex is where a copy of the famous *Bubishi* is believed to have been kept prior to WW2, when this temple too was destroyed. The *Bubishi* was treasured by the martial artists of the *Naha* area, and was of course very influential upon Miyagi Chojun *sensei* who chose the name for his school from a passage contained within the text. The *Merindo* building within the complex is believed to have been the first formal school in Okinawa, providing an education in Chinese studies for children lucky enough to come from a background able to finance such an education. As we walked through the grounds I began to think about how Miyagi *sensei* and Higashionna *sensei* would almost definitely have trod this same ground. This is a very important thing to consider when you visit the island, for it is this connection that allows you to better appreciate the history and really feel a part of it, rather than just reading about it all in a book. History is a living thing, it's something you must see, hear, smell, feel and taste....

We headed west toward the *Budokan* to meet Geiche, choosing to follow the narrow backstreets rather than the main roads which are overgrown with huge soulless concrete buildings. In the backstreets you still have a chance to see the odd classical home, defiantly standing against 'progress' which again allows you to connect a little with a time long since passed. At the *Budokan* we stopped by the monument dedicated to the founder of *Shotokan*, Funakoshi Gichin *sensei*. Not for the first time, I was struck by the apparent lack of thought which had gone into its positioning. Carelessly shoved on the side of the road next to a convenience store and the main road, the site offers no calm place for contemplation, and you have to carefully dodge the traffic in order to get a decent photograph.

With the vast grounds of *Onoyama* Park a mere stone's throw away, it's quite strange why they chose to place it there? Anyway......

Geiche arrived, and together we drove south toward *Itoman*. The landscape soon changed from the grey concrete mess of Naha City, to rolling fields full of sugar cane and rocky elevations leading toward the ocean. Arriving an hour later at the Okinawa Prefectural Peace Memorial Park, we exited the vehicle and began to explore. This was my first time at the Peace Park, and it had been on my 'to do list' for a long time. There are lots of memorials dotted around the huge park, many generously donated by local businesses. Unfortunately there were no English translations available so I did not know what many of them were commemorating. We made our way up the hill toward the coastline, heading toward a place called Mabuni Hill. This was the site made famous by the mass civilian suicides of women and children during the American assault on the island. For anybody unfamiliar with what the Okinawan people went through as a result of the war I would strongly, strongly urge you to read about the Battle of Okinawa. Such things are truly beyond comprehension and I cannot imagine living through such an ordeal. According to the museum literature, 1 in 3 Okinawans were killed during the Battle of  Okinawa. Think for a moment about how many people are in your family and put this in perspective. The whole area around Mabuni Hill is littered with small caves where Japanese soldiers would have been hiding in amongst the frightened civilians seeking safety from the artillery shells raining down upon the island. Any children who cried out were reportedly killed by the Japanese soldiers hiding in the caves in case they betrayed their position. Standing inside these dark, damp enclosures is a haunting feeling, and is probably the most deafening silence I've ever experienced. There is a certain energy about the place which leaves the skin tingling. Many of the trees are still covered in battle scars including the odd bullet hole, as are the rocks which line the route down to the shoreline. Down on the beach we were struck by the beauty of the place, which really betrayed its past history. Looking back up the hill, I wondered what the American soldiers would have felt seeing the climb

and the challenge which appeared before them, knowing that danger was hidden under every rock, and death around every corner?
We all lost ourselves for a little while here, locked away in our own thoughts. I wondered a little way down the beach to perform a *Sanchin* facing the waves. It was all rather melancholic. Not in a horrible way at all, just kind of.......I don't know. I guess you have to experience it yourself to understand what I'm getting at?

We went inside the museum, which was fascinating, and watched many of the videos showing the devastation of the battle and the effects upon the civilian population. The museum describes the buildup to war, the battle itself, and then the post war history of Okinawa and its eventual reversion to Japanese control. As we left the museum to return outside, a Chinook helicopter flew low overhead. The timing of this was impeccable and it really hit home that this whole thing is reality for the Okinawans; not something you read about, but something which many of them have experienced directly and lost family and friends as a result. As the cornerstone of peace, Okinawa sends a clear message to the rest of the world about the stupidity of conflict and the waste of human life which always results.

## **Breathing The Same Air**

Today was our last training session with Hokama *sensei* at the *Kenshikan Dojo*. The Russian *karateka* were also in attendance and had set up video cameras in all four corners of the *dojo* to record the events. I've never been comfortable recording my training sessions and I rarely even take photographs. The general attitude and behavior of these particular visitors had been bugging me ever since their arrival. In the *dojo* they would sit around watching while Mark and I swept the floor, made tea, cleaned up afterwards, and performed various small jobs for Hokama *sensei*, just because this is what you do. I also got quite fed up with being continually used as a human *makiwara* for their benefit whilst they recorded the whole thing rather than actually train themselves. The constant presence of video cameras also appeared to cause Hokama *sensei* to hit harder and hold pain compliance for even longer, eager to impress whoever he imagined would see the video upon their return home. He would regularly complain about them to Mark and me over breakfast, but then pander to their every requirement and demand during the day. I gathered that they had some sort of connection with the Russian government and this is why they were such important visitors, for they were securing Hokama *sensei's* passage to Moscow for a seminar in a few months' time and he was keen to give a good impression. In my simplistic view I thought it would be far easier to turn them all away rather than be irritated by them all week as Hokama *sensei* clearly had been. This is easy for me to think though as I don't have any of the problems that come with running a large *dojo* or association. Despite continually complaining about them during the time they were visiting, Hokama *sensei* decided to promote all three men to a higher grade at the end of their stay. I found this all quite disappointing.

The training this time focused upon *Sanseiru kata*, a personal favorite of mine, and for each technique we were asked to first demonstrate our own ideas about the application for the movements which would then prompt some discussion from Hokama *sensei*, who would then offer his opinions on how to make the same application more effective by incorporating *Kin'na* and *Kyusho*. The results were always extremely painful and most often resulted in me rolling around on the floor screaming at the top of my voice whilst banging the floor repeatedly in an effort to tap out. Such behavior only seemed to prompt Hokama *sensei* to apply the technique even harder and for longer. I'm sure it would have been great fun to watch, but as the person being demonstrated upon it was no joke! Despite the hardship, the session provided much food for thought and we came away with lots to work on. I really like the way Hokama *sensei* teaches *bunkai* in that he doesn't usually give you any new applications, but prefers instead to work with the ones you already have, tweaking them slightly so that they work better. If you have practiced a particular application repeatedly to make it instinctive and built a good all round understanding of it, this approach is much better because the memory process is bypassed and you end up with a better version of the same technique. As somebody who hates the approach of 'collecting more', I find this method of teaching suits me very well.

Following training we made our way back into *Naha* so that our whole group could have lunch together for one last time as Clarke *sensei* and Mitch were due to return home that evening. Finding a small Okinawan restaurant near to the Higaonna *dojo* in *Makishi*, we sat around a table together to talk a lot and laugh a lot. So much had happened in such a short space of time and the trip had moved at such a fast pace that it was difficult to fully appreciate things as they were happening. This for me would require time and reflection, which would only occur once we had returned home. After lunch we strolled around the markets of *Heiwa Dori* to buy some *Omiyagi* (souvenirs) and take in the sights, sounds and smells of the busy market one last time. I got some great little bits for the home and *dojo*; my own little bit of Ryukyu in the UK.

We said our goodbyes and our two groups went their separate ways for the last time in Okinawa. Soon we would once again be on opposite sides of the globe, but still training under the same sky. I like to think of the sky as my *dojo*, for training never seems so lonely this way as I know that somewhere my friends will be echoing the sound of an empty hand striking against a *machiwara*.

Barrett *sensei*, Mark, and I spent the rest of the afternoon walking around *Tsuboya*, looking at the various pottery and antique stores, stocking up on design ideas for our return home. I particularly enjoy walking around *Tsuboya* as Miyagi *sensei's* garden *dojo* was located in this area following the war. As I walk the streets I think of all the famous *Goju Ryu* masters who would have once trod upon this same stretch of ground on their way to visit their teacher.

As the evening drew, Mark and I left Barrett *sensei* for the night and took the monorail back to *Shuri*. We had one last thing to do on our final evening in Okinawa. *Shurijo* is an entirely different place at night. Devoid of all the crowds which appear during the day, you can be sure of a bit of

quiet and solitude at night. We surveyed the panoramic view of *Naha* in full illumination. How this view must have changed over the past 100 years. Still, it was a great view, and I always enjoy this particular sight the most at night. We walked the parts of the grounds which were not closed off and the imagination has a much better chance to roam during the evening whilst the castle is bathed in an eerie glow. Stopping by the small bridge crossing the *Ryutan* pond at *Enkakuji* Temple, we put down our bags and each performed *Sanchin* on the bridge. Although the bridge and the temple, like pretty much everything else on the island, were destroyed during WW2, you can feel safe in the knowledge that the ground it stands upon and the air that surrounds it will be the same as they were all those years ago. As a *karateka*, I find it almost impossible to not want to train in places of natural beauty. There is something about the martial arts which lends itself perfectly to being practiced whilst surrounded by nature. I wonder if this is something peculiar to me or whether it is something which is felt by all martial artists? Anyway, as I looked at *Enkakuji* that night, I was convinced that every famous *karateka* I had ever read about would have looked upon that same site and wanted to train there. As I performed my *Sanchin*, I breathed the same air and trod the same floor as Miyagi Chojun *sensei*, Higashionna Kanryo *sensei*, Aragaki Seisho and Kojo Taite. As I thought of this lineage and considered my place in the chain, I was struck by how *Goju* is a microcosm for life itself. The transition between hard and soft, *yin* and *yang*, inhalation and exhalation, life and death; all of these things describe this art we follow. As I finished *Sanchin* I thought about how it had existed for that brief moment, but was now gone forever. Perhaps sometime soon somebody else would come along and allow the *kata* to live there once again for a short time?

**Reflections**

We awoke early having already packed the night before and said our farewells to Hokama *sensei*. The trip had been an education for me regarding my *karate* and the future direction I wanted to take it. I felt that I had a better understanding of what was and what wasn't important to me this time around, and certain incidents which occurred had left me feeling a little disillusioned with *karate* and all the nonsense that often comes with it. Meeting Kinjo *sensei* again had been the best thing I could have hoped for as he provided me with that much needed affirmation that the things I wanted from

*karate* could be achieved; he was living proof of this.

Leaving the *dojo* one last time, we made our way to *Shuri* Monorail Station in order to head into *Tomari* to meet with Barrett *sensei* and drop our bags at the *Ryokan* he was staying. We had no plan today other than to jump on a bus heading north and see what happened.

Getting on the first bus which was heading up the Route 58, we settled down and chatted about the past couple of weeks. So much had happened and now finally we had a bit of time to reflect and enjoy. We drove past the huge American bases at *Futenma* and *Kadena*, continuing up north until we spotted a sign for *Ryukyu Mura*. I had visited here in 2001 and remembered it as being well worth a visit, so we exited the bus and paid the small entrance fee. *Ryukyu Mura* is a small village complex which represents the architecture and way of life in the old *Ryukyu* Kingdom, offering a time capsule to experience how Okinawa will have looked during the days of Higashionna Kanryo *sensei*. We were really lucky with the weather and had a great time at this unplanned stop, witnessing traditional Okinawan music, food, *bingata* and pottery, as well as learning a little more about the culture, courtesy of the various information boards dotted around. I had by this point developed a real love of the garden styles and various plants and flowers of Okinawa, and was imagining all of the things I could do to my small garden upon my return home. Although we left before the show started, there are also demonstrations of *Eisa*, Dancing, *Karate* and *Kobudo* at *Ryukyu Mura*. Sitting down looking at the large *Koi* pond, enjoying an iced sugar cane drink whilst listening to the sound of a *Sanshin*, I could think of no better place to be.

We left and got back on a bus heading further north up Route 58 towards *Nago*, this time stopping off at Moon Beach. The sea around here is so blue that it is difficult to tell where the sea finishes and the sky begins. We all lost ourselves for a little while here, taking a swim, exploring the various caves and rock formations dotted along the beach, or simply enjoying the view of the horizon. As I mentioned previously, nature lends itself perfectly to training. In the various secluded areas of the beach, we each took some time to practice *Sanchin* and *Tensho*, overlooking the sky blue water. As my gaze hovered over the horizon, the flow of the water back and forth was hypnotic and extremely relaxing, allowing me to enjoy the *kata* even more so than usual. Even now when I perform *Tensho* I can still imagine that same movement of the sea, which allows me to calm my thoughts and move toward stillness.

The entire day had been totally unplanned, but a brilliant way to spend our last few hours in the home of *Karate*. I don't think I'll ever forget the view from that beach, and this will be my lingering memory of Okinawa.

I hope that you have enjoyed this series of articles and sharing our experiences of the trip. Visiting Okinawa is a must for any serious student of Okinawan *Karate*. It is not about the training really, for there are a few places all around the world which can allow you to experience this without the need to travel so far. What this can't provide however, is the experience, the culture, the challenge of leaving your comfort zone, and the memories. If we consider ourselves part of a tradition, it is important to find out where that tradition has come from, to experience the past and encounter the culture in an effort to better understand the context from which our art evolved. Such a trip will always be full of highs and lows, this is life. It is only upon returning to familiarity that you can appreciate just how much you gained from such experiences. I was very lucky this time to share my trip with friends, but do not shy away from the challenge of doing it alone for this brings about an entirely different experience and is equally worthwhile. Our trip was pretty much unplanned in that we didn't set out a schedule for what we would be doing each day. We all found a *dojo* to train at, and then everything else was done on the spur of the moment. Having said that, there were a few of us who have visited Okinawa a number of times so we already knew what we wanted to see and do. If it is your first time I would recommend the following as must see's;

*Shurijo*
*Kinjo* Pavement
*Shikinaen*
*Fukushuen*
*Karate* Monument Tour and *Karate* Museum with Hokama *sensei*
*Naminoue*
*Tsuboya* and *Heiwa Dori*
Okinawa Prefectural Peace Park in *Itoman*
*Nago*, or as far North as you can make it for the landscape differs dramatically from *Naha*!

There are places now offering *Karate* packages which appear a very easy way of experiencing the island. In *karatedo* there is no easy! Your trip, like your *karate*, will be what you want it to be. Get away from the crowds, take control of your own destiny and make it happen. You won't regret it!

# An Interview With Richard Barrett Sensei

For many years I have wanted to interview my teacher Richard Barrett *sensei*, but as anybody who knows him very well will appreciate, he is not particularly forthcoming when it comes to matters which involve him being the center of attention. In fact, to this day, the only time that I have ever seen him perform an entire *kata* was when we were in Okinawa and Kinjo Seikichi *sensei* asked us all to perform a *kata* for him one at a time. My teacher is usually far too private to ever 'show off' in such a way.

As I have said before, many of the ideas which found their way onto the pages of the articles in this and my other books came from various discussions that I had with my *sensei*. I say discussions, but actually these usually consisted of me listening while he talked and I would then steal his ideas and write them down. I always learnt a lot from these discussions and enjoyed greatly hearing about his experiences in Okinawa, training with Miyazato Eiichi *sensei*. Having never had this opportunity myself, I used these stories to appreciate what such experiences must have been like and tried to extract the lessons contained within them. It is my hope that through this interview, other people will be able to find equal inspiration and value in their *karatedo* through the advice and opinions of my teacher.

**GL:** How did you come to first be involved in *Karate*?

**RB:** I first started training during the Bruce Lee boom. In 1974 my father took me to a hired school hall and I started *Kyushindo Karate* which I believe was started in England by Kenshiro Abe, a famous *Judo sensei*. The class was led by a brown belt instructor but because it was quite large, green belts taught the beginners and the brown belt taught the rest. Training was twice a week and I think that this was how most people started their *karate* training back in the 70s in England. One year later I found *Goju ryu* at another town only 10 miles from my house and became hooked on this style. This was also being taught by a brown belt, but the classes were much smaller and *goju* was quite new to England at that time.

**GL:** What prompted you to first travel to Japan?

**RB:** I visited Japan for the first time in 1981, travelling to Tokyo and the *shurinkai dojo* of Morio Higaonna *sensei*. In England I was a member for a short period of the I.O.G.K.F, and as a keen student I went to any course that was open to me to better my *Goju Ryu*, but on a few occasions my instructors, in my opinion, let themselves down. One time an 'instructor' had a display in his office of his 'trophies', which were ladies underwear! Another 'instructor' during a class taught us the value of correct breathing and then after training retired to the bar for a smoke! Some people found these examples funny, I found them sad, and I also found it hard to call these people '*sensei*'. I knew that there must be more to *karate* than this. I had read whatever books I could find and they all pointed to more, but I wasn't finding it in England so my search took me to Tokyo.

**GL:** What were the biggest challenges presented to you during your time in Tokyo?

**RB:** In the early 80s there wasn't the internet as we have it now or email, or even much information about where to go or how to get there at all. I booked an open flight at a travel agent with a Russian Airline to Tokyo, wrote a letter to the *dojo* and another letter to the *kimi ryokan* hostel to book a room, but never got a reply from either of them. I bought a map of Japan and another of Tokyo, and when the time came, a friend and I packed our rucksacks and set off. Friends of mine had gone one year

earlier and gave us a lot of verbal advice, but when we landed in Japan we may as well have landed on another planet. Somehow we made it to Tokyo Central train station with thousands of black haired shorter people marching all around us. All the signs were in *kanji* and we hadn't got a clue about anything!

We looked at one another and seemed stuck yet we had only just arrived! We stood there for what seemed an eternity.

Thankfully a kind Japanese gentleman saw these two lost *gaijin* and helped us with his pigeon English to find where we hoped we would be staying. For two young men, this and all the other trials that we came across during this trip made the whole experience one big learning curve. The *dojo* was the one place that I felt at home. Everything we had to do for ourselves was a real test, we had no one to help us, and everything that happened until we arrived back at Heathrow airport two months later was an experience.

**GL:** Could you please describe what the training was like at the Yoyogi *Dojo* under Higaonna *sensei*?

**RB:** The training was extremely hard. Back in England we thought we trained hard but this was different in that I probably tried too hard and didn't pace myself. As a consequence I would run out of steam after about 40 minutes. The training consisted of *junbi undo,* then *kihon* from *heiko dachi,* always 100 techniques, followed by 100 push-ups and then maybe 100 *uke waza,* followed by 100 sit-ups. This was followed by *kihon ido, mae geri ,mawashi geri,* etc, followed by squats. Then *kote kitai, sandan gi* or *kumite,* and possibly followed by repetition of a *Kata.* The pace of the class was much faster than I was used to and I remember trying my best to avoid doing so, but inevitably looking up at the clock only to find that I still had another hour left to survive.

Morio Higaonna *sensei* was in his 40s and extremely impressive, very powerful looking, and we all wanted to be able to replicate his technique. The classes were all identical, and I did always question myself on the way to each class, asking myself did I really want to do this? Experiences like this, I now know, do help to mold you as a person; you just don't feel like that at the time (laughs). I left training in Tokyo with the advice to put on more weight as during *kumite* I was regularly flattened by the seniors as I only weighed 10 ½ stone at the time. I also grew a lot more confident from the whole journey, but I still hadn't found what I was looking for.

**GL:** What led you to Okinawa and the *Jundokan dojo*?

**RB:** I went to Okinawa four years later, after being promoted to *sandan* in England with the I.K.U. The reason for my visit was that from my studies I had gained a lot of questions and I thought that the answers must be in the birth place of *goju ryu* . So I booked an open ticket to *Naha* Okinawa, this time with China Airways.

Armed with another map, I first stayed at the *Naha* Youth Hostel and within a day or so, found the *dojo* of the Yagi family. In Okinawa at the time there was, to my knowledge, 3 main groups of *goju ryu;* each headed by the three main students of Miyagi Chojun *sensei*, namely the Higa *dojo,* the Yagi *dojo,* and the Miyazato *dojo.* This was what I believed at the time and I knew that Morio Higaonna had come from the Miyazato *dojo* so I decided to try another type of *goju ryu* in the form of the Yagi school. I went to some classes there for the first two weeks of my stay in Okinawa, training twice a week, and the students and teachers were all very friendly. The *goju* was a little different in flavor to what I was used to, but something happened that didn't sit very well with me which caused me to leave. It was implied to me that, should I continue with them, I could become a *yondan* and their European representative! I guess some peoples egos would have flattered by this, but I didn't go back.

I had gone to Okinawa with one student and a friend who didn't train but wanted a two week holiday. My student had started training at the *Jundokan dojo* of Miyazato *sensei*, and so I also made my way there.

**GL:** What particular challenges were presented by the training at the *Jundokan*?

**RB:** Well it wasn't what I expected. I thought it would be similar to the training that I had done in Tokyo, but my student had indicated that it wasn't. I turned up at the *jundokan* and was first taken into a small office and interviewed. Miyazato *sensei* asked me where I was from, how long had I been training and with whom, etc. After this I was told to get changed and was soon stood in front of Miyazato *sensei* wearing a white belt. He asked me to perform *geksai dai ichi* and afterwards he commented that it was "too fast" and about certain techniques he said "why's Morio doing it like that?" This straight away was a new experience for me, one to one training with Miyazato *sensei*! Also, I had always been told "faster, stronger" up until this point, but never to slow down before!

Training in the *jundokan* was a completely different experience for me. It's been well documented about how there was an open training policy, with the *dojo* being open from 10am to 10pm. You could come and go as you pleased, but this was completely new to me at the time. All of my previous classes had always been in a group with a teacher barking out the orders and everybody else responding. People leading, people following.

**GL:** Who were the people who impressed you most, and why?

**RB:** Miyazato *sensei* was the most impressive, but not just because of his technical abilities, which were of course great; it was more his aura and personality which I really admired. I mentioned before some of the things that were new to me in the way that the *jundokan* didn't have a formal class as such, but imagine the *dojo* full of *karateka*, from children through to people in their 70s, all different grades training together under the same roof. The higher grades helped the lower grades and then returned to their own training and what struck me the most was that they were all ordinary people.

Let me elaborate. Up until then, all of the top teachers I had been taught by were professionals. While you or I worked for 8 hours every weekday, they could if they wished, train. They were professional athletes and as a result, were very good, and very fit. All of the students and seniors in the *jundokan* worked or went to school during the day before they came for training, unless they were retired like Miyazato *sensei*. They were normal people, so when I saw seniors there with better technique than mine, I knew that it was also accomplishable for me because they were in the same situation as me. This encouraged me that with a lot of hard work, my technique might one day become as good as theirs.

**GL:** What was so special about Miyazato *sensei*?

**RB:** *Sensei* had a very unique character. In the *jundokan* he was completely in charge; when he asked, students ran, and when he spoke everybody listened. Both inside and out of the *dojo* he didn't suffer fools. He was strong willed, but also had a kind heart. He encouraged the students who he could see had brought enthusiasm to the *dojo* and ignored those that

hadn't. He was very kind to me, in feeding me quite often and also taking me on shopping excursions and visits to different sightseeing locations; none of which he had to do, but he did anyway. I was nothing special to him, just an English *karateka* with a lot of enthusiasm. He even walked with me to the immigration office and acted as a sponsor when I needed to increase my 3 month visa. I also saw that he encouraged his students to help one another inside and out of the *dojo*, supporting one another where possible. I saw his politeness and humbleness when meeting friends

and seniors, and he seemed a very contented gentleman. Some people have remarked that he was a little gruff or seemed to always be in a bad mood in the *dojo*, but I disagree and thought that he was just serious about passing on Miyagi Chojun *sensei's karate*. I also thought he had a wicked sense of humor.

**GL:** What is your favourite memory of your *sensei*?

**RB:** I have a lot of memories, and some of them have already been told through Mike Clarke *sensei's* writings as we shared some of the same experiences together. One time Mike and I were training together in the *jundokan* and we had been put with Yasuda *sensei* one afternoon for him to correct our *kata*. A couple of days earlier Yasuda *sensei*, Mike and I had passed a Kentucky Fried Chicken outlet, and outside was a life sized plastic replica of Colonel Sanders. Yasuda *sensei* joked that Mike looked just like him. Back in the *dojo* our *kata* training had started to get humorous with Yasuda *sensei* saying that Colonel Sanders' *kata* needed a lot of polish. Miyazato *sensei* wandered over, asking what was so funny, and Yasuda *sensei* replied in Japanese "nothing" to which Miyazato *sensei* grunted and walked away. Five minutes later there was more laughter from the three of us and Miyazato *sensei* returned and barked something in Japanese at Yasuda *sensei*, who then bowed his head down and the training together was brought to a close. I think Mike ended up cleaning one area of the *dojo*, while I cleaned another (laughs). Who said Miyazato *sensei* didn't have a sense of humor? I bet he had a good chuckle to himself over that.

Another time I was training with Miyazato *sensei* watching me. I was moving though a particularly fast part of a *kata* when *sensei* suddenly stopped me and corrected a small detail before then walking off. I couldn't believe how he could have seen that the detail was wrong, at speed, but he could. I came to learn that *sensei* would always do his best for me and expected nothing in return. This spoke volumes to me about the type of person he was, and the type of person I would like to call my *sensei*.

**GL:** You also practiced *kobudo* at the *Kodokan dojo* of Matayoshi Shinpo *sensei*. How did this come about?

**RB:** While I was in Okinawa, I met a French *karateka* whilst visiting the Shureido martial arts shop. He spoke English and after a long chat he invited me to go with him to watch a class at the Matayoshi *dojo*, the *Kodokan*. After watching this class I was invited to join. I had previously trained for a short time in Inoue *sensei's kobudo*, so the handling of most of the weapons was not that strange to me. I attended twice a week for about 5 months and as a result got graded in secret to *shodan*!

**GL:** What was Matayoshi *sensei* like as a teacher?

**RB:** Matayoshi *sensei* didn't teach much, or at least I never saw him unless there was someone special arriving at the *dojo* and then he would appear and take charge. The classes were usually taken by one of his top students Oshiro Zenei *sensei*. He was also a *goju* practitioner and spoke some English. I liked his personality and enjoyed the training with him. Matayoshi *sensei* was very kind in that he invited the French student and me to sleep in his *dojo* and set up our beds in a room next to the training area. So we kept the room clean and tidied the *dojo*, and this helped us both with our expenses.

**GL:** What were the biggest lessons that you learnt from your experiences in Okinawa?

**RB:** As I said earlier, I came to Okinawa with many questions and I got a lot of the answers; the answers to the rest of the questions though, I would have to find out for myself. The biggest lessons that I learnt from Okinawa were that *karate* is for everyone who brings enthusiasm to their training, and that there are those who practice *karate* and others who study it. Also, I leant a lot about *karate* and its values outside of the *dojo* by observing and integrating with the Okinawan people. Even during my last visit, the courtesy shown by some of the Okinawan people I found to be wonderful, especially in this day and age where courtesy seems to be a dying art.

**GL:** You returned to the *jundokan* in February 2011. Had the *dojo* changed much since the passing of Miyazato *sensei*?

**RB:** To be honest, I wasn't looking forward to training in the *jundokan* this time around. The thought of Miyazato *sensei* not being there made me feel as if the *dojo* would be empty and I missed him. So I was more focused on going with students, meeting up with old friends, and enjoying the people and culture of Okinawa. Training was at the back of my mind but I was dragged to the *dojo* by Mike, and as I met up with old friends and started training it was great. Training in that *dojo* has always been special for me. Practicing with equipment that was once used by Miyagi Chojun *sensei* and practicing your *kata* on a floor where thousands of others have polished theirs is always special and I hopefully will never take that for granted. Things had changed at the *dojo*, but they always had done, with students leaving and new ones starting with every visit I made. Also, I too had changed. Like life, nothing stays the same, nor should it.

**GL:** In 2001 you founded the *Shinsokai*. What is the purpose of this group?

**RB:** When I left Okinawa the first time I asked Miyazato *sensei* permission for my group in England to become a branch *dojo*. Ahhh, I wish I'd never asked! Miyazato *sensei* became very serious and told my *sempai* Chinen Shinzo that we would have an interview in half an hour at a local restaurant. *Sensei* disappeared upstairs and my *sempai* and I got changed, with Chinen *sensei* telling me "it will be alright." I must have looked very worried. The solemn interview came and went with questions such as "what do you think *karate* is?" and "how would you teach *karate* in England?" Well, Miyazato *sensei* left, and Chinen *sensei* was still telling me "it will be ok." The following day at training I was asked to perform all of the *goju ryu kata* in front of *sensei* and other seniors, and then when that had finished, I was packed off in a car to Hichiya *sensei's dojo* to do the same again in front of him. The next day training was back to normal until *sensei* called for everyone to line up and he presented me with my *yondan* certificate. Also before I left Okinawa, *sensei* gave me another certificate entirely in Japanese, and it wasn't until I was back in England and had it translated that I found out I was now in charge of England! I thought that I had just been granted permission for a small branch *dojo*.

That year I wrote a couple of articles and advertised, and over the next couple of years I started to assemble a group of *dojo* under the banner of the *Jundokan* G.B. I held courses and once a year we held a *gasshuku*. I tried to encourage the *kuroi obi kai* to study their *karate* by asking them to do book reviews and write essays regarding *karate*. For some of them, this went down like a lead balloon! They were only interested in the external, but I didn't care; quality not quantity had always been my motto and I hoped that they would just leave. But as time passed, I found that I was becoming attached to the title of 'chief instructor' and my ego, rather than getting smaller, was increasing. So, as soon as I had realized this, I made the decision to let it go and gave up the title to someone who needed it. A couple of years later in Okinawa, Miyazato *sensei* told me I had been brave to give up that position.

10 years ago I formed the *shin so kai*, just before I left to immigrate to Spain with my family. This was mainly to give the students I was leaving behind a bond of unity. I know that some of them thought I was abandoning them, but now I think that they would agree that it has made them better *karateka* for it. Throwing them out of the nest so to speak.

5 years ago I stated to get a lot of excuses rather than reasons from some members in England and I decided that some drastic action was needed, so I threw all the members out of the *shinsokai*, emailed them all asking if they would like to re-apply and then only excepted the students who wanted to study *karate* without excuses.

The *shin so kai* name is made up of three characters. Working backward '*kai*' is a group of people. '*So*' is 'searching/looking for something with bare hands' which I thought appropriate for *karate*, and '*shin*' means 'truth' or 'realty'. So the purpose of this group of like-minded people is to find, though the medium of Okinawan *goju ryu karatedo*, the truth of their own nature to then better enhance their own life. Everybody is an individual and lives within their own set of circumstances, and I hope that though the study of *karate* they will come to know themselves a little better and will come to understand others around them too. They can then go on to make educated decisions for a better life.

**GL:** What would you say is the main focus of your teaching?

**RB:** To deliver the above. I think there is a minority of educated people who have discovered for themselves that a person is not more important than another because they have a bigger house or a nicer car, or because they wear designer clothes, are better looking or even famous. Hopefully this minority has discovered that what 'makes' a person is their personality.

From when I first started *karate* I read that within the art there was woven a set of moral codes that we should all aspire to, but as I mentioned before, there are a lot of *karateka* who are not interested in being a good person; only kicking, punching and titles. Over the years I have seen and heard of a lot of bad examples, but these examples can only confirm to me that I don't want to travel down that same path.

I try to veto any members that want to join these days, and if a student gives me any reason to doubt their conduct, then I would tell them they are no longer welcome. I tend to believe these days in peoples actions and non-actions rather than what they say.

**GL:** What is your opinion of the state of *Goju Ryu* today?

**RB:** Well, most people just want to learn and practice the physical side of *karate*, but then others add to that by learning about the history and culture of Okinawa, and studying the precepts that underline *karatedo*. All of these people will receive some benefit from this, even if it's just improving their level of fitness.

I believe that the true benefit of practicing *karate* is being able to put what you learn to some use. What's the point of learning how to fight when you never intend to, and will probably never actually have a fight, unless you go looking for one of course? I would say that 95% of people who practice *goju ryu* around the world today only do so at a superficial level. It doesn't matter how long they have been practicing or what grade/title they have either. But that's ok, *karate* is for everyone.

*Karate-do* is a little different though. Some people search for more from their *karate* and get tired of just following the leader. They will hopefully find a *sensei* and *dojo* that can help them make *karatedo* a part of their life.

**GL:** Where do you see *Goju Ryu* in another 20 years?

**RB:** Much the same as it is now I guess. Hopefully, there will still be small pockets of practitioners just practicing, but I don't think that true training in *goju ryu karatedo* will ever be a big affair. It can't be, it's an individual pursuit and requires a level of personal guidance that is quite intimate.

**GL:** How do you think *karate* is still relevant today?

**RB:** I can only speak about my own personal experiences. When I wake up in the morning, I try to remember to be very grateful. I am very thankful for having a loving wife and two, sometimes, wonderful children (laughs). I have my health, and I am content with what I have. This I believe has been possible because of my training in *karate*. Not the fact of having a wife and children, but the appreciation of what I have, and what a wonderful way to start the day. I believe that through proper training, *karate* can give the student a wonderful insight in to what is and what isn't important in life as they come to understand more about themselves.

**GL:** What is the most important aspect of *karate*?

**RB:** Your attitude to your training. If you don't have that, then you will gain very little from your *karate*. First of all, you will always need the enthusiasm to want to improve, but also honesty with yourself so that when things start to get hard you don't start making excuses. Courage and being determined are also good attributes, but as I said earlier, everyone is different and *karate* will enhance the character attributes that are lacking in a person to then hopefully help them to develop a balanced personality.

**GL:** Do you have any final thoughts to finish this interview?

**RB:** At this moment in time I am 'digging out' the fourth *dojo* that I have personally built (**note:** this *dojo* is being literally dug out of a small cave in the hillside behind Barrett *sensei's* home!). I have traveled to Japan several times and other locations on this planet in pursuit of bettering myself as a *karateka*. I built my own kit car with the help of my brother. We immigrated to Spain with the hope of bettering our lives and with the help of my wife Claire, we rebuilt from a derelict basic shell of a house, the place we now call home. Claire owns and runs a health food shop and Community Center in our local town and enjoys giving her time to the people who need it, and I am very proud of her. I have been training in *karate* for nearly 38 years and still find its pursuit a challenge. I do not want my students to equal what I have achieved, I want them all to surpass me and exceed what I have learnt and done. This does not mean that I expect my students to start moving country or building a house (laughs), but I would like them to study *goju ryu karatedo* and though it, all find and enjoy a contented life. I don't consider myself very clever or intelligent, just ask my wife (laughs), but I do know that life's too short, and the sooner you take control of your own unique situation and steer it in a good direction, the more contented you will become with what you have and who you are.

# Personal Formation Through A Study Of Karate-do

## Jinkaku (personality, character)

Why do you study *karate-do*? Everybody has their own unique reasons which cause them to be attracted to practicing *budo*. Some people want self-defense, improved fitness, increased confidence, superiority over others, a means of income, a competitive outlet, or an enjoyable pastime which can be conducted a couple of times a week to escape from everyday life. Although such reasons may initially bring a person to the door of *budo*, few of these reasons will remain should the person persevere with their practice for any reasonable length of time. The reasons for practicing *budo* change over time, and with each change, new issues arise to confront the practitioner. Through the course of our journey in *budo*, we will be brought into direct confrontation with our own true nature.

A person entering through the door of *budo* will on many occasions possess either a *Go* or a *Ju* type personality, and each has its particular merits and problems. How would you describe your own character in these terms? A person's reasons for initially studying *budo* can also be classified as either *Go* or *Ju*, and this can give some indication about the type of personality they bring with them. *Karate-do* presents the challenge of then helping to achieve balance in a person's character so as not to be too *Go* or too *Ju*. Both are required in equal amounts to create a balanced person.

The *kanji* relating to *kaku* means 'character' or 'rank'. The rank translation is interesting as this suggests some kind of status which is naturally inherent within our personalities. A person with an overly *Go* personality can often see themselves as being 'above' or more important than others, and can be dominant and selfish in their nature. A person with a predominantly *Ju* personality can view themselves as being 'beneath' others, has a subservient manner, and is often too eager to please. The trouble is, most often, a person will not even be aware of this type of self-imposed rank structure, and can remain ignorant for their entire life, unable to reach their full human potential. The job of the *sensei* is to notice these traits at the earliest opportunity in a student, and then tailor the training to provide sufficient challenge in order to bring these personality traits to the surface so that they can be seen by the student. For many people, this will be the first time they will actually meet their true nature.

## Hinko (conduct, behavior, actions)

The teacher who has recognized certain traits in the student will often present opportunities to 'wake up' along the path of training. These take the form of various tasks or challenges and can be either overtly challenging in nature, or extremely subtle, requiring attentiveness and a thirst for improvement from the student for the lesson to be recognized.

How the student approaches such opportunities will be watched and assessed carefully. How they perform the task itself will also be monitored closely, as will the student's attitude once the test is completed. The *kanji* relating to *Ko* means 'going, do, conduct, or exercise'. This implies that a person's character can be revealed through the performance of a task. The terms *Hinko* and *Jinkaku* are closely related it seems.

We all wear many masks throughout life, and the mask we wear often depends upon the social situation we find ourselves in. The Japanese say that a person has two hearts; one that he shows to everyone, and the other which is shown only to family and close friends. This is referred to as *omote* and *ura*, surface, and what is behind or not easily seen. I personally believe that there is a third heart which is known only to ourselves, but many people never become aware of this as they remain too concerned about the heart they show to other people. This third heart can be considered our true nature, or our soul. I think the soul and the spirit are two separate entities. What do you think about this?

Nagamine Shoshin *sensei* wrote that 'there shouldn't be but a hairs breadth between a man's word and his deed'. Richard Barrett *sensei* also says that you should judge a person by their actions rather than their words. The masks that we wear throughout life are often invisible to the person wearing them. This is because they are too attached to them, and unable to remove the masks in order to view them dispassionately. Training in *karate-do* forces a person to remove their mask and take a good look at it. Only then can you really see both the beauty of the details, and any defects which need to be repaired.

*Karate-do* carries with it guidelines to correct behavior, and an ethos which stresses the importance of positive character traits in order to develop people into good human beings and benefits to society. Some of these guidelines can be unpopular as they cause confrontation between what a person **wants** to be, and what they are **expected** to be. It is this confrontation which leads to the wearing of multiple masks as a person tries to please everybody and themselves at the same time. This is why there are so many *karate* authorities these days who say one thing, yet do another. They have unfortunately missed the most important lessons. The confrontation between a person's wants and expectations can take a long time to resolve, and in many cases, perhaps this confrontation is never finished or even started. The challenge of *karate-do* is to develop the ability to wear a single mask of 'truthfulness'. This is what we are searching for with our hands in the *shinsokai*. This truthfulness means not to mislead others into thinking you are somebody you are not, but it also means that we become truthful with ourselves and recognize our own characters; all parts of it, good, bad and ugly. Once we can be honest with ourselves about who we really are, the hard work can begin in sculpting our personalities into objects of beauty. A sword begins its life as a piece of dull earth which is not impressive or particularly useful in its natural state. By going through the process of continual forging, its natural qualities emerge, and are further refined. At the end of this process, the sword is robust and useful, perfectly adapted to its intended purpose. At this point, the sword is then polished, and its visual elegance hides its superior ability to perform its intended task well. What is the intended use for your *karate-do*?

## Jinpin (character, personality, appearance)

Although on the surface this phrase appears similar to *Jinkaku*, a look at the *kanji* reveals that they are in fact quite different. The *kanji* relating to *Pin* translates to imply 'elegance, grace, refinement and dignity'. The difference between the two terms can be likened to the useless piece of earth going through the process of transformation to become a sword.

The most respected *karate* masters of old were known equally for their physical skill and their strength of character. *Karate* was the pursuit of the upper classes, and the appearance and behavior of its practitioners reflected strongly this noble heritage. A persons social standing and reputation is considered very important in Okinawa, and during the times of the Ryukyu kingdom this was something which was reflected through all levels of society, hence Okinawa being internationally referred to as 'the land of propriety'. Tome Pires, a Portuguese medical expert who travelled extensively around Asia in the early 1500's wrote admirably about the Ryukyuan's stating;

*"As we ourselves talk of Milan and those from there, the Chinese and other peoples talk of the Lequios (Ryukyuans). They are very truthful men. They do not buy slaves, nor would they sell one of their own men for the whole world. They would die over this. They are white men, better than the Chinese and more dignified. They sail to China and take merchandise that goes from Malacca to China, and from Japan. This is an island about 7 or 8 days by sea from their island. There they buy the gold and copper in exchange for goods. The Lequios are men who freely extend credit for their merchandise. And when they come to collect their payments, should they be lied to, they collect with sword in hand."*

Miyagi Chojun *sensei* spoke of his dislike of street entertainment performances such as *tameshiwari*, or the breaking of objects over the body. He described such acts as being vulgar. His choice of words is quite lofty, and indicative of his noble background. He was known to be a hard taskmaster, and his daughter recalled how much attention he paid to simple matters such as the length of ones fingernails. Old photographs reveal how immaculate his appearance was at all times, and his posture is always attentive and proud. An old Okinawan saying is that 'you should spend words as wisely as you would spend money', meaning that you should be careful not to be wasteful. Through being reserved and refined in our speech and appearance, we limit the opportunities for carelessness, and the danger of causing unintended offense. By being mindful of good manners, courtesy, how our actions affect others, and recognizing opportunities to do something good, we bring happiness to other people, and have a positive influence on society. Negativity causes further negativity. Personalities influence other personalities, so a cheerful, helpful disposition can assist others who may be feeling down. This is good for humanity and good for the soul.

## Jinryoku (human strength)

Everybody is born with human potential and the ability to achieve greatness, but few people realize their natural strength, wasting their time on frivolous activities which they believe will bring them happiness but ultimately lead nowhere. Walking the path of *budo* allows sufficient opportunity to challenge yourself and overcome your own self-imposed limitations. The human body is capable of far more than we give it credit for, and most of the time the spirit will fail before the body gives up. Through setting challenges and achieving goals which you thought beyond you, we learn to trust ourselves and develop *Jishin* (self-confidence). *Jishin* allows us to realize our human potential, and gives us the courage to reach for our goals and press forward with an assertive attitude. Through going through this process, we strengthen our ability to counter negativity with positivity, looking optimistically at whatever problems are presented. We learn to develop patience and an understanding that immediate results are not always possible; but despite this, we do not lose heart, and keep striving forward with determination and the knowledge that with continual effort we will achieve victory. A person equipped with such an attitude becomes useful in society, and such individuals emerge as natural leaders, capable of motivating others.

## Ningen Keisei (personal formation)

This can be said to be the ultimate aim of *budo*. Although on the surface, the martial arts address ways of fighting and dealing with conflict; at their core they are no different from any art where raw materials are transformed into something useful through a long process of careful attention to detail and polishing, such as carpentry, sculpture, or painting. The tools and raw materials on their own lack purpose and have limited use. Through the process of coming together under the expert eye of the master craftsman, the raw materials are altered by the tools so that their outer appearance changes into something admirable, and they become useful, with a strong purpose in life. When this is achieved through *budo* then this is a truly wonderful thing. The raw material possesses *Jinryoku*, but without the correct use of the tools, they cannot achieve this hidden potential. Likewise, the tools on their own are useless and serve no purpose. In addition to this, if the tools are used by an unskilled or careless craftsman, the end result of the raw materials might not be particularly good, and in some cases, a craftsman of dubious character might even create something capable of causing harm or injury to other people.

All three areas are equally important. The raw materials must be of good quality and not contain too many natural imperfections which could later interfere with the transformation process. The tools must be sharp and well maintained so that they are able to perform well for the craftsman. The craftsman must be attentive, and possess the vision to look past the obvious and into the very soul of the raw material so that he is able to bring its *jinryoku* to the surface. As you can see, all three elements are mutually beneficial and provide the ideal circumstances for art to flourish.

## Jinseikan (outlook on life)

Our way of viewing the world is shaped by our personal circumstances, family background and upbringing, peer groups, occupation, and economic standing in life. Things like religion, nationality, gender and sexuality also play a large role in this. For a person who dedicates themselves fully to the *budo*, it is inevitable that their outlook on life will be shaped by their experiences in the *dojo*. Depending upon what is done inside the *dojo*, this can either be a very good thing, or an extremely negative thing. I have seen numerous examples of people who take themselves too seriously, or view every situation as an opportunity to prove themselves as tough. Equally I have seen remarkable examples of *karateka* who literally go through life without anybody noticing they are even there. Although the *budo* may have enormous value to us as individuals, in the grand scheme of things, they are only one way of approaching a problem. There are many other ways in the world which can achieve similar outcomes through an entirely different process of human development. By following the way, we learn to relate all matters to our training. If the training has sufficient balance, this is a great way to approach life, and you might find that you are able to avoid some of the common dangers which befoul so many people. I think it is no coincidence that the *budoka* who I admire most have been able to create personal lives which are enriched with happiness, and void of the common problem of always wanting more. Materialistic nature, greed, and desire, fall by the wayside as we become more focused upon the important things in life, knowing instinctively what is necessary for us to achieve contentment.

### Jindo (humanity)

By developing a deep understanding of ourselves, we ultimately learn compassion and empathy for other people. Through coming face to face with our own uncertainties, character flaws, and weaknesses, and stripping away the masks to view our true face; we come to understand that this is not something which is unique to us, but that it applies to all humankind. We see that if such frailties can be found within ourselves, other people will also be vulnerable to the same flaws. Such an understanding removes conflict, and develops the ability to remain emotionally unattached to a problem. With such detachment, we can then view a problem rationally and avoid reacting impulsively.

Through an in-depth study of *Bu* (War), we ultimately come to an understanding of *Wa* (peace). This is the essence of *karatedo*.

# **Conclusion**

I sincerely hope that you have found something of worth within this modest work to help you along your path of *karatedo*. Some of the articles are a little confrontational in asking you to take a good look at yourself and the art you practice; others might seem a little 'mystical' in nature, as I have also been accused of this in the past. The fact is, people all learn and respond in different ways, and what helps one to person understand can sometimes be quite useless for another. The key is to not rely upon the information you are given, but to test it for yourself and find your own understanding of what works for you. I personally respond to imagery and visualization, so 'flowery' wording and descriptions help to inspire the correct feeling in my technique. Due to this, I explain things in this manner. I hope that certain messages do not get lost behind this.

If this book achieves nothing other than helping to deliver the message that with a little determination and the will to do a little of something every day, you can achieve your goal; my work will have been worth the effort. Continuity is power, so keep moving forward one pace at a time.

*Karatedo* can be many different things to different people, but I sincerely hope that the majority can find more than just the physical techniques and matters relating to fighting, for these are only the superficial rewards. The real treasures of this beautiful art can only be found when we learn to look beyond the physical or any external opponent, and start to explore our true nature. This has been written about so many times over the years, but until we develop an intimate understanding of this ourselves, it remains just words.

Thank you very much for taking the time to read this work. I wish you the best of luck in your training.

*Garry Lever*
*March 2012*
*London, England*

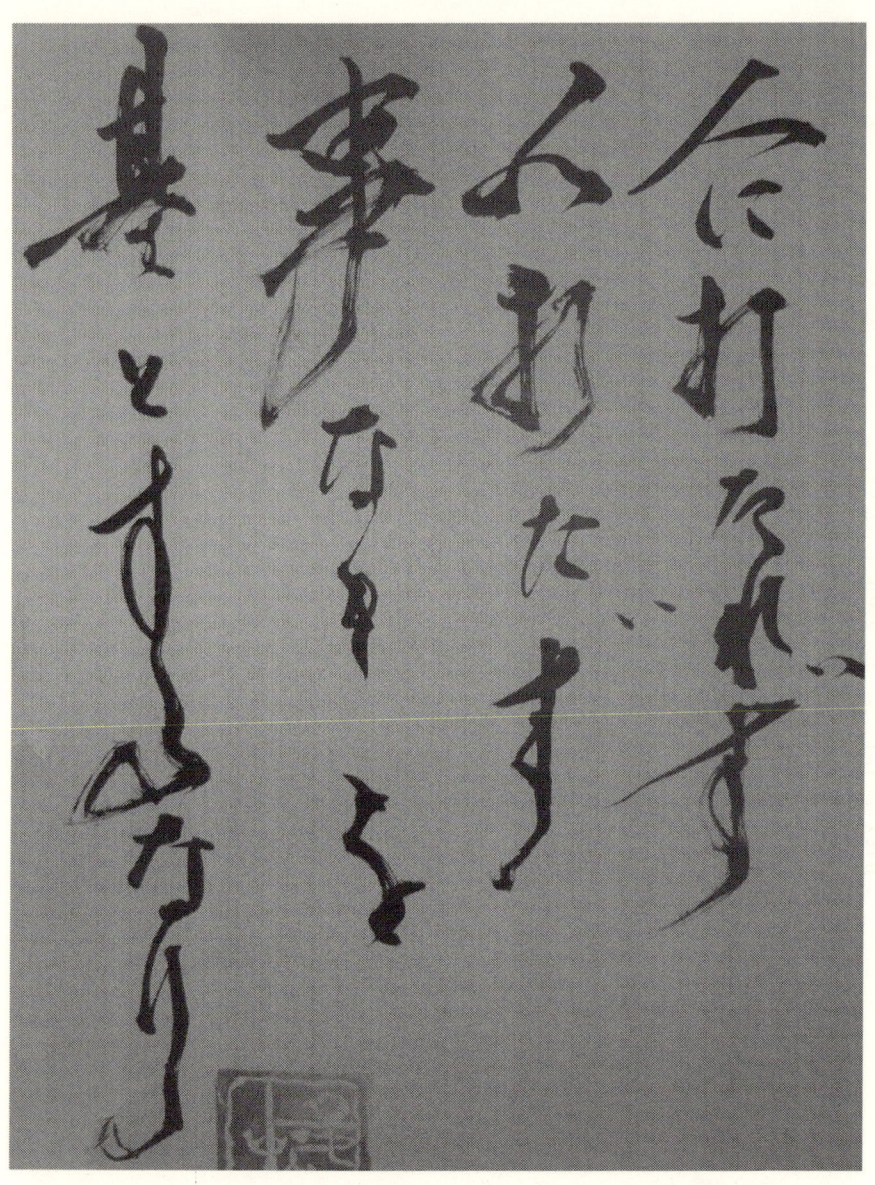

*Do not strike others; do not be struck by others. This is the principle of peace without incident.*

**Miyagi Chojun sensei**

(brushed by Hokama Tetsuhiro sensei)

## Glossary

| | |
|---|---|
| *Budo* | Martial Way |
| *Bujin* | A person devoted to the martial arts |
| *Bujutsu* | Martial arts |
| *Bunkai* | To take apart and analyze |
| *Busaganashi* | Martial arts deity |
| *Bushi* | Respected warrior |
| *Chiishi* | 'Strength stone' hojo undo implement |
| *Do (Dao)* | The way |
| *Do-gi* | Practice uniform |
| *Dojo* | 'Place of the way' where practice is conducted |
| *Dojo Kun* | Moral precepts found in classical dojo |
| *Goju Ryu* | Hard Soft School founded by Miyagi Chojun sensei |
| *Hojo Undo* | Classical strength training |
| *Ishi Ganto* | Marker stone used to ward off evil and bring good fortune |
| *Jinryoku* | Human power |
| *Jissen* | Real fighting |
| *Junbi Undo* | Preparatory movements |
| *Jundokan* | Dojo established by Miyazao Eiichi sensei |
| *Kamae* | Posture |
| *Kaki Dameshi* | Term used to refer to a challenge match |
| *Kakie* | Pushing hands training |
| *Kanji* | Chinese characters used in writing |
| *Kansetsu Waza* | Joint techniques |
| *Kappo Jutsu* | Resuscitation methods |
| *Karamidi* | Entangling hands (restraining and arrest techniques) |
| *Karatedo* | The way of the empty hand |
| *Karateka* | Karate practitioner |
| *Kata* | Pre-arranged forms |
| *Kazushi* | Breaking of posture |
| *Kenko* | Practice geared toward health benefits |

| | |
|---|---|
| *Kensei* | *Fist Saint* |
| *Kin'na Jutsu* | *Joint locks and nerve attacks often referred to as Tuidi* |
| *Kobudo* | *Ancient martial ways* |
| *Kohai* | *Junior practitioner* |
| *Kumite* | *Lit crossing hands* |
| *Ma'ai* | *Distance of engagement* |
| *Machiwara* | *Striking post used for conditioning* |
| *Miyagi Chojun* | *Founder of Goju Ryu* |
| *Miyazato Eiichi* | *Founder of the Jundokan Dojo* |
| *Mokuso* | *Quiet contemplation* |
| *Muchimi* | *Heavy sticky action* |
| *Naha* | *Capital of Okinawa* |
| *Nahadi* | *Lit Naha Hands (commonly refers to the martial arts of Naha)* |
| *Obon* | *Festival of the dead* |
| *O-Tsuna Hiki* | *Tug of War event held annually in Naha* |
| *Oyo* | *Personal interpretation of application* |
| *Qi (Ki)* | *Vital energy* |
| *Rei* | *Courtesy (commonly attributed to the act of bowing)* |
| *Ryukyu* | *Chain of islands stretching between Japan and Taiwan* |
| *Sanchin* | *'Three Battles' kata* |
| *Sanshin* | *3 Stringed classical Okinawan instrument* |
| *Seiken* | *Hand formation striking with largest two knuckles of the fist* |
| *Seiza* | *Kneeling posture* |
| *Sempai* | *Senior practitioner* |
| *Sensei* | *'One who has lived before' teacher* |
| *Shinshi* | *Okinawan (uchinaguchi) term for sensei* |
| *Shinzen* | *Dojo shrine* |
| *Shisa* | *Guardian lions* |
| *Shodo* | *Brush calligraphy* |
| *Shomen* | *Focal point of the dojo* |
| *Shuri* | *Ancient capital of the Ryukyu Kingdom* |

| | |
|---|---|
| *Soji* | *Cleaning* |
| *Suidi* | *Lit Shuri Hands (refers to martial traditions of Shuri)* |
| *Tanden* | *Focal point located below the navel* |
| *Ti* | *Lit Hand. Indigenous Ryukyu martial art (precursor to karate)* |
| *Tomari* | *Famous harbor town near Naha* |
| *Tomaidi* | *Lit Tomari Hands (refers to martial traditions of Tomari)* |
| *Tuidi* | *Joint manipulation and nerve attacks* |
| *Uke Waza* | *Lit receiving techniques (refers to blocking movements)* |
| *Uraken* | *Back fist* |
| *Yoi* | *Preparatory kamae and mental state* |
| *Zanshin* | *Lingering awareness* |
| *Zazen* | *Meditation* |

Also available by the author;

Wondering Along A Dark Path
&
The Essence of Goju Ryu – Vol 1

Made in the USA
Lexington, KY
30 November 2014